C++ Programming

Complete guide to learn the basics of C++ programming in 7 days

By

Xavier S Martin

© **Copyright 2020 by Xavier S Martin- All rights reserved.**

The content contained within this book may not be reproduced, duplicated or transmitted without direct written permission from the author or the publisher.

Under no circumstances will any blame or legal responsibility be held against the publisher, or author, for any damages, reparation, or monetary loss due to the information contained within this book, either directly or indirectly.

Legal Notice:

This book is copyright protected. It is only for personal use. You cannot amend, distribute, sell, use, quote or paraphrase any part, or the content within this book, without the consent of the author or publisher.

Disclaimer Notice:

Please note the information contained within this document is for educational and entertainment purposes only. All effort has been executed to present accurate, up to date, reliable, complete information. No warranties of any kind are declared or implied. Readers acknowledge that the author is not engaged in the rendering of legal, financial, medical or professional advice. The content within this book has been derived from various sources. Please consult a licensed professional before attempting any techniques outlined in this book.

By reading this document, the reader agrees that under no circumstances is the author responsible for any losses, direct or indirect, that are incurred as a result of the use of the information contained within this document, including, but not limited to, errors, omissions, or inaccuracies.

Table of Contents

INTRODUCTION 9

CHAPTER 1: INTRODUCTION TO C++ 10

1.1 Background of C++ 10

1.2 C++ Programming 11
- *How to write a C++ program* 11
- *Simple Program* 12
- *Hello World* 12

1.3 Constants 15
- *Integer Constants* 15
- *Character Constants* 16
- *Float Constants* 17
- *Boolean Constants* 17
- *Programming Constants* 18

1.4 Data Type 20
- *void (Void)* 20
- *int (Integer)* 20
- *char (Character)* 21
- *bool (Boolean - logical data in C++)* 21
- *float (Floating Point)* 21

1.5 Variables 22
- *Variable Initialization* 22
- *Variable Declaration* 23

1.6 Programming Examples 23
- Problem 1 23
- Problem 2 24

1.7 Exercise Sets 25

CHAPTER 2: HOW TO WRITE A C++ PROGRAM 27

2.1 Expressions 27

- *Primary Expressions in a C++ Program* 28
- *Binary Expressions in C++* 29
- *Assignment Expressions* 32
- *Postfix Expressions* 36

2.2 Statements 38
- *Expression Statement* 39
- *Compound Statement* 41

2.3 Programming Examples 42
Problem - 1 42
Problem-2 44

2.4 Exercise Sets 45

CELSIUS = (100 / 180) * (FAHRENHEIT - 32) 46

CHAPTER 3: CONCEPT OF "FUNCTIONS" IN C++ 47

3.1 Structured Programming and Designing 47

3.2 Functions in C++ 49
- *User Defined Functions* 50
- *Function Definition* 51
- *Prototype Declaration* 53
- *Function Call* 54
- *Void Functions with no Parameters* 56
- *Void Functions with Parameters* 57
- *Function Example* 57

3.3 Default Parameter Arguments 59

3.4 Programming Examples 60
Problem - 1 60
Problem - 2 61

3.5 Exercise Sets 63

CHAPTER 4: SELECTION-MAKING 65

4.1 Logical Data and Operators 65

- *Logical Data in C++* 66
- *Logical Operators* 66
- *Evaluating Logical Expressions* 69
- *Relation Operators* 71

4.2 Two Way Selection 72
- *If, Else* 73
- *Rules for If Else statements* 73
- *Null Else Statement* 76
- *Nested If Statements* 79

4.3 Multiway Selection 80
- *The Switch Statement* 80
- *Else If Statement* 81
- *Example Program* 81

4.4 Menu Program, C++ 83
Problem 83

4.5 Programming Examples 84
Problem 84

4.6 Exercise Sets 97

CHAPTER 5: CONCEPT OF "ARRAYS" IN C++ 98

5.1 Using Arrays in C++ 98
- *Declaration and Definition* 99
- *Accessing Elements in Arrays* 99
- *Storing Values in Arrays* 99
- *Inputting Values* 99
- *Assigning Values* 100
- *Exchanging Values* 100
- *Putting Value* 100

5.2 Arrays and Functions 102
- *Passing Individual Element* 102
- *Passing the Whole Array* 102

5.3 Array Applications 103
- *Frequency Distribution Arrays* 103
- *Histograms* 104

5.4 Sorting 106
- *Selection Sort* 106
- *Insertion Sort* 108
- *Bubble Sort* 109

5.5 Programming Examples 111
Problem - 1 111
Problem - 2 112

5.6 Exercise Sets 113

CHAPTER 6: CONCEPT OF "POINTERS" IN C++ 115

6.1 Pointers 115
- *Pointer Constants* 115
- *Pointer Values* 116
- *Pointer Variables* 117

6.2 Accessing Variables through pointers 117

6.3 Pointer Declaration 118

6.4 Initialization of a Pointer Variable 119
Problem-1 120
Problem-2 122

6.5 Pointers and Functions 123
- *Pointers as Formal Parameters* 123
- *Functions Return Pointers* 124

6.6 Arrays and Pointers 125

6.7 Programming Examples 126
Problem - 1 126
Problem - 2 128

6.8 Exercise Sets 129

CHAPTER 7: CONCEPT OF "CLASSES" IN C++ 130

7.1 Classes 130
- *Access Specifiers* 131

- Creating a Class 132
- Declaring a Class 132
- Class Definition 133

7.2 Defining a Class Object 135
- Instantiation 135
- Accessing Class Members 135
- Using Classes 137

7.3 Constructors and Destructors 137
- Constructors 137
- Destructors 139

7.4 Programming Examples 141
Problem - 1 141
Problem - 2 142

7.5 Exercise Sets 143

CHAPTER 8: CONCEPT OF "STRINGS" IN C++ 145

8.1 Strings 145
- Fixed Length String 146
- Variable Length String 146

8.2 C++ Strings 147
- Storing Strings 147
- String Literals 147

8.3 String Input/Output 148
- String Input ">>" 148
- String Output "<<" 149

8.4 Array and Strings 151

8.5 Compare Packed Strings 152

8.6 Morse Code Program Design 153

8.7 The String Class 155

8.8 Programming Examples 158
Problem 158

8.9 Exercise Sets 161

CONCLUSION 162

REFERENCES 164

Introduction

C++ is a computer programming language widely used for general-purpose programming. It is an extension of C-language. The basic understanding of C++ can be acquired from C. That's why both computer languages are represented as C/C++. Bjarne Stroustrup developed this multi-paradigm language in 1979.

In today's world, many operating systems use C++ as their basic language. Some system drivers, browsers, and games are based on C++ programs. It is a free-form, compiled, and statically-typed programming language. Many professionals believe that C++ is the most efficient language to achieve the desired results.

In the "Complete guide to learn the basics of C++ programming in 7 days", I have covered all the essential basic concepts for beginners. It is a step by step guide, which makes sure the understanding of C++ programming. First of all, there is a need to know the structure and syntax of C++, along with the basic expressions. Then, it guides the major "Functions" such as mathematical manipulation and Standard Library. Moreover, there are complete guidance about the selection making of operators and logical data, concepts of Arrays, Pointers, Classes and Strings in C++.

While there are so many great programming languages, but C++ is the most favorite owing to have the privilege of the first Object-Oriented Programming language. Nowadays, there are several high-level languages with simple syntax and user-friendly options. Still, programmers can't deny the importance of C++ because of its huge number of open-source libraries, wide applications, and highly fast run-time performance.

This guide is designed for beginners who want to learn C++ in 7 days. You will discover this language by making your programs while reading this book.

Chapter 1: Introduction to C++

In the following chapter, we will discuss about the evolution of computer programming languages and their evolution from machine languages.

As we know C++ is a high-level language. We'll discuss the concepts of C++, in this chapter. Moreover, you will be able to write your first program, after going through this chapter, i.e. "Hello World". Furthermore, you'll understand the concepts of Constants, Variables, Data types and some of the operators that may help you writing and understanding a C++ program.

1.1 Background of C++

C++ is considered a properly structured programming language, that's why this is so popular. C++, as you know, is a high level language because it allows a programmer to concentrate on the problem at his hand, without worrying about the system that the program may be using. There are many languages who claim to be system or machine independent but C++ is one of the best among them.

Like many other languages, C++ is basically derived from ALGOL, which was the first language to have a structure. ALGOL was developed in the early 1960s and it made a path for structured programming and its concepts. Very first work in ALGOL was done by two scientists name as Guiseppe Jacopini and Corrado Bohm. Both of them published a research in 1960 which defined a thorough idea of structured programming.

In 1967, a computer scientist named as Martin Richards designed a language designed a programming language; he named Basic Combined Programming Language aka. BCPL. In 1970, Ken Thompson developed a language, known as "B". Following him, Dennis Ritchie, in 1972, developed the concept of language "C".

Following all the concepts from the languages, ALGOL, BCPL, B and C, Bjarne Stroustrup, developed C++ in mid 1980s.

1.2 C++ Programming

Now, when you know about the background of C++, i guess, you'll be eager to write your first program. This section will let you know the basic parts of a C++ program, so that you'll be able to write your very first program.

- *How to write a C++ program*

First of all, we need to understand, the "Global Declaration". Your program is considered a little world; a world of computer universe. So, we may start our program with global declaration.

Secondly, only one function, in your program must be named as "main". Main is the starting of the basic program, after global declaration. Main can have two kinds of code;

- **Declaration**

Declaration is considered the data that you may use to justify or write your program or function. If you declare something in a function, it'll be known as "Local Declaration". We call them local declarations because they are read, only be the function itself.

- **Statements**

Statements are some commands to the machine that is using the program. Statements cause the machine to perform the actions, such as adding or subtracting numbers, multiply them, taking their average etc.

- *Simple Program*

We know that C++ allow us to make declarations and statements at the same time, but, every time, we should write a program, which should be well organized so that any other programmer or even the machine could understand it fast. This is the reason, we follow the language C's concepts of organization. The concept states that one should perform declaration first and statements second. Moreover, most of the times, one should use comments for the identification of the sections; Declarations and Statements.

A C++ program is a mixture of two components main (Main) and fun (function). In other words, function is called or used by main. Usually, we write the code for the "main", first. After that, we'll code the function and sub functions, in their order.

Moving forward, there is another concept; concept of preprocessor directives or precompiler directives. These are some statements which give instructions to a compiler or processor to execute the program in a unique pattern.

A statement which is globally used as a preprocessor directive is, "include". This statement allows the compiler to extract some data from global libraries, known as header files. Without these header files or libraries, you will not be able to write even a single program, because it'll be so complex to write the commands even for your input or output. Even, you will need an "include" command, to write your very first program. This will be used to instruct C++ that you will be in need for the input and output libraries, so that you may print your desired data to the console screen.

- *Hello World*

Your first C++ program is going to be very straightforward. It will include just one precompiler directive and no global or local declaration would be made. It will just display a greeting to the user on a console screen. Because this program is not so complex, it will contain only two statements; first, to display a greeting, the second one would be used to terminate our program.

We will write the precompiler directive in the very beginning of our program. Precompiler directives must start with a number sign i.e. "#", in any C++ program. The syntax for our precompile directive would be:

#include <iostream.h>

In this precompiler directive, we may write # first and there should be no space between "#" and "include". Statement "include" will include the concerned library in your program, which will be mentioned in the pointed brackets "<>".

In the following statement, "iostream" is a short form for "input output stream" and ".h" is to represent header file.

Moreover, we'll use another statement in our program which is:

using namespace std;

For understanding this statement, we have to consider a classroom with a boy and a girl; sharing the same name and class, but having different functions. So, when you will call their name, both will respond. The very same confusion can be a part of programming, as if there is a function named as "poi()" and in some other library there is another function named as "poi()", your compiler would not be able to identify your desired function. To overcome this difficulty we usually use this statement.

Moving forward, our program's executable part would be starting with a function header, such as:

Int main (void)

For this statement, we have to understand that the "int" states that this specific function will send back an integer value to the machine or operating system.In the concerned statement, our function's name is "main" and it has no specific parameters, as we have voided the parameter list with "(void)".

Now, there are two more statements, with first, we will be able to print our desired data. And with the second, we will be able to terminate the program.

cout << "Hello world";

This statement is used to display or print the desired data, in this case "Hello World". This statement uses an operator "<<", this operator allows us to print or display data in our console. This statement contains inverted commas "". Whatever, you will be writing in these commas, will be displayed in your console.

Finally, the program will be terminated with a statement:

return 0;

This statement will simply end the program and will hand over the control to operating system again.

Now, if you need to write your program, you'll need a compiler first. There are many compilers available, online and offline, to execute your code in C++. If you need to compile your code offline Turbo C++ and Dev C++ are highly recommended and if you need to compile your code online, you may search for any online C++ compiler.

Typically, the first program is known as "Hello World", but we'll change the odds. We will be writing our first program as "Hello to the world of C++!"

So if you have a compiler now, you are all set to write your very first program. We'll start with header files and then the body of program and we will terminate it with our termination statement.

So, your first program should look something like this:

#include <iostream>

using namespace std;

int main()
    {
        cout << "Hello to the world of C++!";
        return 0;

}

When you'll execute this program, there will be a console screen popping up with the text:

Hello to the world of C++!

We've already written our first program so now, we will be discussing some more important concepts of programming in C++.

1.3 Constants

The concept of constants in programming is very similar to the concept of constant in Mathematics. Constants are the values or data which remains unchanged during the execution of a code or program.

In this section, we will define different types of constants in programming.

- *Integer Constants*

First thing first, integers are stored in binary formation. You'll code integers, as you use them in your daily routine, for example you will code eight simply as 8.

The following table will show you different integers, their values in programming and their data types

Value in programming	Number	Data Type
98	+98	int
-865	-865	int
-68495L	-68495	long int

| 984325LU | 984325 | unsigned long int |

- *Character Constants*

Whenever, you'll find an integer, closed between two single apostrophes, this would be character constant. Moreover, there is a chance that you'll find a backslash "\" between those apostrophes.

For most machines, ASCll character set is used, i.e.

ASCII Characters	Symbolic Display
Null character	"\0"
newline	'\n'
horizontal tab	'\t'
alert (bell)	'\a'
backspace	'\b'
form feed	'\f'
vertical tab	'\v'
single quote	'\''
backslash	'\\'
carriage return	'\r'

- *Float Constants*

Float constants are stored as two parts in memory as float constants are numbers having decimal parts. The first part, they obtain in memory is significand and the second is exponent.

Float constant's default type is "double". You must write a code to specify your desired data type, i.e. "float" or "long double". We may remember that "f" or "F" is used to represent float and "l" or "L" is used to represent long double.

In the following table, some of the examples of float, double and long double.are shown:

Value in Programming	Number	Data Type
.0	0.00	double
0.	0.00	double
3.0	3.0	double
5.6534	5.6534	double
-3.0f	-3.0	float
5.6534785674L	5.6534785674	long double

- *Boolean Constants*

These constants are predefined keywords and they can not be defined or declared by the programmer. It has two predefined constants, "True" and "False". In programming, we represent this kind of constant as "bool".

- *Programming Constants*

In this part, we are going to understand different programming constants, and ways to write and define constants in a C++ program. Usually, there are three types of programming constants.

- **Defined Constants**

A way to define a constant in a C++ program is to use a precompiler statement "define". Like every other precompiler directive, it starts with a "#". For example, a traditional precompiler directive for "define" would be:

#define TABLE_SIZE 150

Define directives are usually placed in the beginning of the program, so that anyone reading your program, can find them easily.

- **Memory Constants**

Another way to code constants is by using a memory constant. These constants use a C++ type qualifier to remember that the specified data can not be changed.

C++ programming provides us with an ability to define named constants. We just have to add type qualifier in our code, before constant. For example:

Code:

#include <iostream>

using namespace std;

#define val 50

#define floatVal 9.7

#define charVal 'K'

int main()

    {

        cout << "Integer Constant in our code: " << val << "\n";

```
        cout << "Floating point Constant in our code: " << floatVal << "\n";
        cout << "Character Constant in our code: "<< charVal << "\n";
        return 0;
}
```

Output:

In the case of this code, a console screen will pop up with the output:

Integer Constant in our code: 50

Floating point Constant in our code: 9.7

Character Constant in our code: K

- **Literal Constants**

Literal constant is a constant which is unnamed and used to specify your desired data. As we know constant can not be changed so we just have to code its data value in a statement.

Literal constant is the most common form of constant. Here is a table to show different kind of literal constants.

Values	Type
'C'	Character Literal
7	Numeric Literal 7
C + 8	Another Numeric Literal (8)
5.6534	Float Literal
Hello	String Literal

1.4 Data Type

A data type defines a set of operations and values that have the ability to apply on the concerned values. For example, a switch of a light bulb can be compared to a computer system as it has two different values; True as On, and False as off. Since the bulb switch contain just these two values, we can consider its size as two. There are just two operations that can be done with a bulb switch:

- We can turn it On
- We can turn it Off

In a C++ program, functions have their own unique types. Usually, a function's type is specified by the data it returns. C++ usually contains five standard data types:

- void (Void)
- Int (Integer)
- char (Character)
- bool (Boolean)
- float (Floating Point)
- *void (Void)*

In C++, void has no operations or no functions. In simpler words, both the set of operations and the set of values are empty. It is a very useful data type in programming although it seem unusual. Typically, it is a generic data type that can represent any other standard data types.

- *int (Integer)*

In C++, integer is a number without having a fraction part, we usually call it an integral number. Our concerned language supports three types of integers as its data types:

- **short (Short Integer)**

- Int (Integer)
- long (Long Integer)

C++ allows us to use an operator "size of", that may tell us the size of our data types. Whenever, we are coding in C++, we should keep this statement in mind:

sizeof (long int) => sizeof (int) => sizeof (short int)

- *char (Character)*

We usually think of characters as the alphabet or numbers, but programming has its another definition. By this definition a character can be any number, value or symbol that can be represented by the machine or computer's alphabets.

Moreover, we have to remember that C++ usually treat characters as an integer because it uses memory as an integer i.e. between 0 to 255.

- *bool (Boolean - logical data in C++)*

Boolean data types has two functions, True and False. Traditionally, a zero is considered as false and any non-zero part is considered as true.

- *float (Floating Point)*

Float data type or floating point is usually a data type having a fractional part. When coding in float data type, we should always consider this statement:

sizeof (long double) => sizeof (double) => size of (float)

We may think that the data type, float and data type, integer are the same, but there are many differences as the "float" is always declared in a C++ program.

Data Types	Implementations
Void	void

Integer	Unsigned short int, unsigned int, unsigned long int, short int, int, long int
Character	char
Floating point	float, double, long double
Boolean	bool

1.5 Variables

Variable, in C++ are memory locations, having different data types, such as character or integers. Variables are manipulatable and changeable because the use a set of different operations.

- *Variable Initialization*

By using an initializer, we can declare and initialize a variable at the very same time. Basically, initializer set up the variable's very first value. Usually, an identifier is followed by a "=" sign to first initialize and then define a variable's initial value, when the function starts. Simple syntax of initialization is:

Int count = 0

Moving forward, we have to keep in mind that whenever a variable is defined, it is not automatically initialized. The programmer should be the one to initialize any variable, when the program starts.

- *Variable Declaration*

Every variable, in a program, must be defined and declared. In C++, we use Definition to create different objects and we use Declaration to name those objects. Whenever a programmer creates a variable, definition reserves memory for it and definition assigns it a symbolic name. Variables, when assigned, hold data that is required by the program to fulfil its task.

In C++, multiple variable of the similar types can be declared in a single statement. Many programmers use this technique but we won't be recommending this as this is not a good programming technique. This reduces the efficiency of program and the efficiency for the execution process of compiler.

1.6 Programming Examples

Problem 1

We read about the ASCII character set, print your desired character ASCII values from A to Z.

Solution:

```
#include<iostream>
using namespace std;
int main ()
{
   char a;
   cout << "Enter your desired character to print its value: ";
   cin >> a;
   cout << "According to ASCII character set, value of " << a <<" is : " << (int)a;
   return 0;
}
```

Output:

When you will execute this program, a console screen will pop up with this text:

Enter your desired character to print its value:

You simply have to type your desired alphabet to print its value. Let's say you want to print the value of "G". Simply type "G" and press "Enter" key. Your program will print the value of "G" according to ASCII character set. It will, somehow, look like this:

According to ASCII character set, value of "G" is : 71

Problem 2

Write a program in C++ that uses five output statements to print the pattern shown below.

A

AA

AAA

AAAA

AAAAA

Solution:

```
#include <iostream>
using namespace std;
int main()
{
  cout << "A"<< endl;
  cout << "AA"<< endl;
  cout << "AAA"<< endl;
  cout << "AAAA"<< endl;
  cout << "AAAAA";
  return 0;
```

Output:

When you execute this code, a console screen will pop us with your desired pattern, i.e.

A

AA

AAA

AAAA

AAAAA

1.7 Exercise Sets

- Write a C++ Program by using "cout" or output statements to print the initials of your name in block letters. Program should not read any alphabet from your keyboard. Each letter should be formed by using seven columns and five rows, using the letter itself. For example if your name is "Faheel", your output should be something like this:

  FFFFFFF

  F

  FFFF

  F

  F

- Write a C++ program to read an integer, character and floating point. Program should print each of these on a separate line.

- Write a program in C++ that allows the user to enter three numbers and them it prints those numbers vertically (one in a line), first, in ascending order and then in descending order, as Shown in below example:

Output:

First, your console should print a line saying:

Please enter any three random numbers:

After entering numbers, let's say 10, 50, 17, it should print:

> **Your numbers in ascending order:**
>
> **10**
>
> **17**
>
> **50**
>
> **Your numbers in descending order:**
>
> **50**
>
> **17**
>
> **10**

Chapter 2: How to write a C++ program

C++ have three unique features that sets it apart from most of the programming languages:
- Expressions
- Pointers
- Classes

In this chapter we will discuss the very first of these concepts, i.e. Expressions. We have already used expressions in Mathematics, but the way to use expressions is unique to "C++" and its precursor "C". The concept of expressions is tied to the concept of precedence, operators, statements and associativity.

2.1 Expressions

Expression, in a C++ program, is a sequence of operators and operands that eventually reduces to a single value. For example, 10 * 2.

In the following example, the expression reduces to 20. In C++, final value can be of any data type, other than void.

- **Operators**

Operators are the language specific syntactical tokens that require some action to be performed. Many operators are derived from the concepts of Mathematics. For example "Sign of Multiplication (*)" is an operator used in C++. It multiplies two numbers.

Every programming language has unique operators to perform unique operations.

- **Operand**

For any defined operator, there may be one or more than one operands. Operand has to receive any operator's action. In above example, (10 * 2), Multiplier and Multiplicand are the operands of Multiplication.

There is no limit of operand sets and operators to form an expression. The only rule is that when program will evaluate the expression, the answer should be a single value, that may represent the expression.

- *Primary Expressions in a C++ Program*

In C++, most initiatory kind of expressions are Primary Expressions.It contains just one operand and no operator. We have to remember that operand can be a name, parenthetical expression or a constant in Primary Expression.

- **Names**

It is an identifier which defines a function, a variable or any other object in C++.

- **Constants**

Another type of primary expressions are Constants.Constants are the pre recognized or declared data whose value is unchangeable during the compilation and execution of a program.

- **Parenthetical Expressions**

Last kid of primary expression is parenthetical expression.It is a primary expression because its value is always reducible to a single value. So, the complex expression in a parenthetical expression may be bound to make it a primary expression.

- *Binary Expressions in C++*

Binary expressions in C++ are typically formed by operand-operator-operand relation. These expressions are the most common. Any two numbers subtracted, multiplied, divider or added are written with the operator between two operands. Or may be in algebraic expressions. Most common types or binary expressions are:

- **Additive Expressions**

First type of binary expressions is additive expressions. In this kind of expression, second operand is added to the first operand or the second operand is subtracted from the first operand. It depends upon the operator, that is used. These kinds of expressions use parallel algebraic notations for example, a + 18 and b - 90. Here are two sample programs to show such kind of expressions:

For Addition:

```
#include <iostream>
using namespace std;
int main()
{
// Declaration of integers
    int firstinteger, secondinteger, sum;
// Printing input and output commands
    cout << "Enter any integer: ";
    cin >> firstinteger;
    cout << "Enter another integer: ";
    cin >> secondinteger;
// Sum of two integers is stored in the variable "sum"
    sum = firstinteger + secondinteger;
// Printing sum of first and second integer
```

```
    cout << firstinteger << " + " <<  secondinteger << " = " << sum;
    return 0;
}
```

For Subtraction:

```
#include <iostream>
using namespace std;
int main()
{
// Declaration of integers
    int firstinteger, secondinteger, sub;
// Printing input and output commands
    cout << "Enter any integer: ";
    cin >> firstinteger;
    cout << "Enter another integer: ";
    cin >> secondinteger;
// Subtraction of second integer from first is stored in the variable "sub"
    sub = firstinteger - secondinteger;
// Printing the subtraction of second integer from first integer
    cout << firstinteger << " - " << secondinteger << " = " << sub;
    return 0;
}
```

- **Multiplicative Expressions**

This expression is known as multiplicative expression because of its first operator, i.e. Multiplication. We consider it on top, in binary expressions. Its value is calculated as the product of two operands, i.e. 5 * 2 = 10.

In such expressions, division is a little more complex. In division if both operands are integers, the result would be the integral value of quotient. It would be expressed as an integer, i.e. 5 / 2 = 2. Here are two sample programs to show such kind of expressions:

For Multiplication:

#include <iostream>

using namespace std;

int main()

{

// Declaration of integers

   int firstinteger, secondinteger, mul;

// Printing input and output commands

   cout << "Enter any integer: ";

   cin >> firstinteger;

   cout << "Enter another integer: ";

   cin >> secondinteger;

// Product of two integers is stored in the variable "mul"

   mul = firstinteger * secondinteger;

// Printing sum of first and second integer

   cout << firstinteger << " * " << secondinteger << " = " << mul;

   return 0;

}

For Division:

#include <iostream>

using namespace std;

int main()

{

```
// Declaration of integers
    int firstinteger, secondinteger, div;
// Printing input and output commands
    cout << "Enter any integer: ";
    cin >> firstinteger;
    cout << "Enter another integer: ";
    cin >> secondinteger;
// Integral value of quotient in division of first integer and second integer is stored in the variable "div"
    div = firstinteger / secondinteger;
// Printing the subtraction of second integer from first integer
    cout << firstinteger << " / " << secondinteger << " = " << div;
    return 0;
}
```

- *Assignment Expressions*

Assignment expression is an expression which usually evaluates the operands on the right side of an equation and automatically places its value to the variable on the left side. There are two types of assignment expressions:

- **Simple Assignment**

Simple assignment is a form of assignment expressions which is present in the form of algebraic expressions such as x = 60, y = n + 20, z = x + y.

The thing to remember, in a simple assignment, is that the left operand should be a single variable. In such expressions, the value of the right side is evaluated and it becomes the value of the entire expression. In the following table there are some examples of simple assignment and how its value is calculated.

Expressi	Value of	Value of	Value of	Result of

on	"n"	"m"	Expression	Expression
n = m -1	20	15	14	**14**
n = m + 20	20	15	35	**35**
n = m * o	20	15	0	**0**

- **Compound Assignment**

Compound assignment is considered as a shorthand writing for the simple assignment. In this case, left operand should be repeated in the right side.

To evaluate a compound assignment, machine first changes it into simple assignment and then performs the operations to identify the final result of the expression.

In the following table, it is shown that how a compound assignment is converted into a simple assignment:

Compound Assignment	**Simple Assignment**
n %= m	n = n % m
n /= m	n = n / m
n *= m	n = n * m
n -= m	n = n - m
n += m	n = n + m

In the following table there are some examples of compound assignment and how its value is calculated.

Expression	Value of "n"	Value of "m"	Calculation of Expression	Result of Expression
n %= m	20	15	n=(20/100)* 15	3
n /= m	20	15	n = 20 / 15	1.33
n *= m	20	15	n = 20 * 15	300
n -= m	20	15	n = 20 - 15	5
n += m	20	15	N = 20 + 15	35

In C++, we use compound assignments as:

For Addition:

```
#include<iostream>
using namespace std;
int main()
{
   int n = 5, m = 2;
//Compound assignment expression n += m means n = n + m
   n += m;
   cout << n << endl;
```

    return 0;
}

For Subtraction:

```cpp
#include<iostream>
using namespace std;
int main()
{
    int n = 5, m = 2;
//Compound assignment expression n -= m means n = n - m
    n -= m;
    cout << n << endl;
    return 0;
}
```

For Multiplication:

```cpp
#include<iostream>
using namespace std;
int main()
{
    int n = 5, m = 2;
//Compound assignment expression n *= m means n = n * m
    n *= m;
    cout << n << endl;
    return 0;
}
```

For Division:

```cpp
#include<iostream>
using namespace std;
```

```
int main()
{
  int n = 5, m = 2;
//Compound assignment expression n /= m means n = n / m
  n /= m;
  cout << n << endl;
  return 0;
}
```

- *Postfix Expressions*

In C++, postfix expressions operates just after the primary expression, followed by an operator.

- **Function call**

Function call is an elementary component in structured programming. Function call is basically a postfix expression. In such expressions, operand is the function's name and it follows its operator. We have to remember that function call always have some value so it can be used in other expressions, except from void.

- **Postfix Increment and Postfix Decrement**

Both postfix increment (n++) and postfix decrement are postfix operators. Usually every program, in C++ require the value 1 to be added in its variable. In most of the programming languages, this can be done in binary expressions.

C++, on the other hand provides its programmer an ability to code this in both binary as well as unary expressions.

In postfix increment, the variable increases its value by 1. So, "n++" is calculated as the variable "n" being increased by "1". This expression is similar as assignment expression:

n++ means that n = n + 1

On the other hand, postfix decrement (n--) also have values and results but in this case, machine reduces your variable (n) by 1 i.e. n - 1.

Postfix Expressions	Value of n (Before)	Evaluation of Expression	Value of n (After)
n--	20	20 - 1	**19**
n++	20	20 + 1	**21**

For Postfix Increment:

#include <iostream>

using namespace std;

int main()

{

  int n, a;

  cout <<"Enter any integer: ";

  cin >> n;

  a = n++;

  cout << "Post Increment Operation:"<<endl;

  // Value of a will not change

  cout << "a = " << a << endl;

  // Value of n will change after execution of a=n++;

  cout << "n = " << n;

  return 0;

}

For Postfix decrement:

```
#include <iostream>
using namespace std;
int main()
{
   int n, a;
   cout <<"Enter any integer: ";
   cin >> n;
   a = n--;
   cout << "Post Increment Operation:"<<endl;
   // Value of a will not change
   cout << "a = " << a << endl;
   // Value of n will change after execution of a=n--;
   cout << "n = " << n;
   return 0;
}
```

2.2 Statements

In C++ any action performed by a program is caused by statements. It translates the executable commands into machine language. In C++ there are six kinds of statements:

- **Expression statement**
- **Compound Statement**
- **Labeled Statement**
- **Iterative Statement**
- **Selection Statement**
- **Jump Statement**

Most important among them is compound statement and expression statement. We will be discussing these two statements in this section.

- *Expression Statement*

In C++, any expression can be turned into a statement, by placing a semicolon ";" after it. Whenever a C++ compiler sees a semicolon, it evaluates the value of expression, saves it in variable and discards it before compiling the next argument or statement. Just consider an expression statement to be:

n = 69

It means that the vale of this expression is 69. The compiler will save the value 69 in the variable "n". After storing 69 in "n", compile will terminate this expression and will discard its value. Then compiler will continue to the next statement. However, the value of "n" will remain stored in "n".

Example Program:

```
#include <iostream>
using namespace std;
int main()
{
    // declaration statement
    int n = 69, m;
    cout << "Enter the value of m: ";
    cin >> m;
    // expression statement
    n = n + 1;
    // expression statement
    std::cout << "n = " << n << '\n';
    // return statement
    return 0;
```

}

A bit more complex statement in expression statements can be:

n = m = 69;

This statement consists of two statements. If we factorize this statement, we will see the expressions clearly

n = (m = 69);

The compiler will assign the value 69 to "m" during the compilation process. After evaluating "m", the compiler will terminate and discard the value of "m" and then will start to calculate the value of "n". After the compiler's execution of this statement, 69 will stored in both the variables "m" and "n".

Moving forward, consider a postfix expression as an expression statement, i.e.:

n++

In this expression, the value of expression is 69. It is also the value of our variable "n", before it is increased by 1. When the compiler will execute the statement, the value of the variable "n" will be 70. But the value of the expression, i.e. 69, will be terminated.

Moreover, we have a special type of expression statement known as null expression. This expression statement has no value and no side effect and this can be very useful in some compex statements. Null expression is represented as a single semicolon.

;

- *Compound Statement*

In C++, a compound statement is a coding unit consists of some statements or no statement. We may also call compound statement; a block. This statement allows many statements to execute as a single unit. While writing your first program, you used a compound statement, i.e. while writing the body of the function main. In C++, every program has a compound statement in it, which we call function body.

Every compound statement have some parts in it, i.e.

- **Opening Brace "{"**
- **Declaration and Definition (Optional)**
- **Statement Section (Optional)**
- **Closing Brace "}"**

As we mentioned that declaration, definition and statement section is optional, but one one them must be present in your compound statement. Otherwise, there would be no need of a block.

As for your first program, the compound statement was:

{ // Opening Brace

    cout << "Hello to the world of C++!"; // Statement

    return 0; // Return Statement

} // Closing Brace

We have to remember that, semicolon, after this statement is not needed. If you place a semicolon after the closing brace, compiler will consider it a syntax error.

Furthermore, we have to remember that we may declare and define a statement anywhere in a block but it makes the program so difficult to read and understand. Declaration and definition of a statement on the top of the block is considered a good programming technique. It allows a programmer to read, understand, rewrite and maintain a C++ program easily. We may also put comments "//" in a block to remember the statements. For example:

```
{ // Opening Brace
    // declaration statement
    int n = 69, m;
    cout << "Enter the value of m: ";
    cin >> m;
    // expression statement
    n = n + 1;
    // expression statement
    std::cout << "n = " << n << '\n';
    // return statement
    return 0;
} // Closing Brace
```

2.3 Programming Examples

Problem - 1

Your program must read four integers from the keyboard, calculate their sum and their average and it should print the answer on the screen.

Solution:

```
#include <iostream>
using namespace std;
int main()
```

```
{
    float n, m, o, p, sum, average;
    cout << "Enter first number: ";
    cin>>n;
    cout << "Enter second number: ";
    cin>>m;
    cout << "Enter third number: ";
    cin>>o;
    cout << "Enter fourth number: ";
    cin>>p;
    sum=n+m+o+p;
    average=sum/4;
    cout << "The sum of " << n << " and " << m << " and " << o << " and " << p << " is: " << sum << endl;
    cout << "The average of " << n << " and " << m << " and " << o << " and " << p << " is: " << average << endl;
}
```

Output:

When you execute this program, a console screen will pop up with a line:

Enter first number:

After entering your desired number, let's say "69", the program will ask for the second number:

Enter second number:

After entering your second number, which is "69", as well, the program will ask for the third number:

Enter third number:

Consider you entered 69 again, as the third number. Program will demand the fourth number:

Enter fourth number:

Just say that you entered 69 again, as the fourth number.

Your program will add all of your entered numbers and then divide their sum on 4. After calculating It will print:

The sum of 69 and 69 and 69 and 69 is: 276

The average of 69 and 69 and 69 and 69 is: 69

Problem-2

Your program must read the temperature in Celsius and change it into Fahrenheit, using the following equation:

Celsius = (100 / 180) * (Fahrenheit - 32)

Solution:

We have to convert this formula manually to find the amount of Fahrenheit. So from

Celsius = (100 / 180) * (Fahrenheit - 32)

We may Calculate:

Celsius = (5 / 9) * (Fahrenheit - 32)

(9 * Celsius) / 5 = (Fahrenheit - 32)

((9 * Celsius) / 5) + 32 = Fahrenheit

Fahrenheit = ((9 * Celsius) / 5) + 32

Now, using this formula, we may write our program.

```
#include<iostream>
using namespace std;
int main()
{
    float fa, ce;
    cout << "Enter the temperature in Celsius : ";
```

```
cin >> ce;
fa = ((9.0 * ce) / 5.0) + 32;
    cout << " Your entered temperature in Celsius : " << ce << endl;
    cout << "Temperature in Fahrenheit         : " << fa << endl;
    return 0;
}
```

Output:

When you execute this program, a console screen will pop up saying:

Enter the temperature in Celsius :

After putting your desired temperature, let's say 78, the program will calculate according to the formula and will give out the output as:

Your entered temperature in Celsius : 78

Temperature in Fahrenheit   : 172.4

2.4 Exercise Sets

- Write a program that reads a measurement in Inches and print the values in
    - Foot i.e. 12 Inches
    - Centimeter i.e. 2.54 / inch
    - Meter i.e. 39.37 Inches
    - Yard i.e. 36 Inches
- Write a program that reads length and width of a rectangle from user and calculates the area of the rectangle.

- Write a program that should read the temperature in Fahrenheit and change it into Celsius, using the following equation:

Celsius = (100 / 180) * (Fahrenheit - 32)

Chapter 3: Concept of "Functions" in C++

We were learning the very basic concepts of C++ till now. The programs, we made were able to perform one, two or a very few tasks, at one time. They were not able to perform too many tasks, simultaneously.

Now, if we consider a larger program, we can not deal with it without breaking it into sub parts.

For example, you have to visit all the museums of some city in a week and then you have to make a report of them. What would you do!

- You will gather data about the museums
- You will calculate the distance between museums
- You will make a route that would suit you
- You will estimate your time

Now, programming of the larger programs follow the same process. At first, you need to understand what the problem is. Then, you may break your larger program into smaller parts or modules. This programming style, basically, is known as structured Programming.

3.1 Structured Programming and Designing

In Structured programming, it is defined that a program must be divided into a few modules and it can be further subdivided into many other modules.

In the following chart, we may learn about how structured programming works:

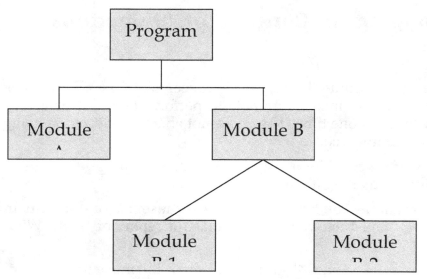

First of all, we have a program that we have to develop. In this case, we break it into two parts, i.e. Module A and module B. Moving forward, Module B is sub dividen in two sub modules, Module B-1 and Module B-2.

So, we can think that Module B-1 and Module B-2 are the smaller parts of Module B and Module A and Module B are the sub modules of a larger program.

Our program will work by calling different modules. For example, if we want module A to send data to module B, Both modules will communicate through the main program. We have to remember that direct communication between two modules is not possible if they don't have a calling-called relationship. Moreover, a module, in structured programming can be called by only one higher module. This allows data to pass through a function and this technique is known as parameter passing.

3.2 Functions in C++

In C++, module and submodules are known as functions. In every C++ program, there should be one or more functions and one of them must be main. Main is the key function, your program must start and end on main and main can call other functions, if necessary.

A function is an independent module that is called to perform some specific tasks. In C++, function can return a value to the caller. In a program, main is called by the OS (operating system), after that main is responsible for calling other functions. When main performs its task, the control then returns back to the operating system.

Generally, the task of a function is to receive data, works on it and returns it in a compiled form. With its pros, function can have side effects as well. A function can change the state of a program.as it may reduce efficiency of a program. Moreover, receiving and returning data to an outside source and to change any variable's value can be a function's side effects.

C++ provides a large use of functions in it as functions can be used to factorize a program. Secondly, functions can be helpful if you want to use the same function in many parts of your program. For example, if you want to calculate the average of five random numbers. So instead of coding all the time, you may develop a function and can call it, whenever you need it.

To understand the coding for functions, we may have a look at this code:

#include <iostream>

using namespace std;

// Function declaration

int mul (int,int);

// Main Function

int main()

{

// **Function Call**

  cout<<mul(1,99);

  return 0;

}

/* Function is defined after the main method */

int mul(int num1, int num2)

{

  int num3 = num1*num2;

  return num3;

}

- *User Defined Functions*

Functions must be declared and defined, like any other object in C++. In C++, we can declare a function by the declaration of prototype. The definition of a function contains a code to perform some specific tasks. We may understand it with this example:

#include <iostream>

// Declaration of Prototype

Int mul (int, int)

Int main ()

{

// Local declarations

....

// Statements

....

// Calling of a function can be done in statements

cout<<mul(1,99);

....

....

return 0;

}

// Definition of a function is done after the calling function

int mul(int num1, int num2)

{ // Statements

   int num3 = num1*num2;

   return num3; // Multiplication

}

- *Function Definition*

The definition of a function is based upon the code for a function. In C++, it has two parts:

- **Function Header**
- **Function Body**

Function body is a compound statement, we have to keep in mind that every complex statement must have an opening brace, declarations, statements and closing brace. The definition of function should be like:

// Function Header

return_type function name (parameter list)

// Function Body

{

// Local Declarations

....

// Statements

....

// Function Name

.....

....
}

- **Function Header**

A function header has three parts:
- Return Type
- Function Name
- Parameter List

A semicolon is not allowed on the end of it, otherwise, there will be a syntax error.

In function header, if the return type is not perfectly coded, the compiler will assume it an integer. If you are not returning anything in your code, you have to code the return type as void.

- **Function Body**

Generally, a function body has two main parts; Declarations and Statements. It starts with local declarations and the declaration of variables. Following the declarations, statements are coded. Statement section ends with a return command. If a function is returning a void-type, It can be written without a return command, but it is a good practice to still use it.

For Example:

// The function's return type have to be defined

int one (...)

{

....

....

....

return (n + 69);

} // First

void two (...)

{

....

....

....

// We have to use a return statement, even if nothing is returned

return;

} // Second

In the above example, the function "one" is declared to return an integer, so its return statement have the expression **(n+69)**.When this statement is compiled, this expression is calculated and the result is returned.

For function "two", it returns nothing. Void is its return type, so it doesn't need any return statement. In this case, it is executed just with a semicolon.

- *Prototype Declaration*

Prototype declarations contain no code and consist of only a function header. Prototype headers are also consist of three parts:

- **Function Name**
- **Parameter List**
- **Return Type**

Unlike the function headers, prototype declarations are terminated with a semicolon. In a C++ program, it is placed before main, in global declaration area.

For parameters, C++ does not require any identifier names, but readability and understandability is increased is you use names for them. We have to remember that if types are not the same, you will receive a syntax error because compiler checks types before compiling a code, so they have to be compatible.

We have to remember that:

- Formal parameters are the variables which are declared in the function header.
- Formal parameters and actual parameters should have the same data type, number and order. However, their names can differ.
- Actual parameters are the expressions in function body's calling statements.

An example for prototype declaration is:

Int add(int 1, int 2);

- ***Function Call***

In C++, function call is always a postfix expression. We have to remember that in primary expressions, postfix expressions are on the highest level. So, if a function is used by a larger program, compiler will calculate and execute it first, until we command it to perform some different tasks first.

In a function call, operand is the function name, which consists of actual parameters. These parameters evaluates and decides the values that are to be sent to call our desired function.

For example:

#include <iostream>

#include <cmath>

using namespace std;

int main()

{

   double n, m;

   cout << "Enter your desired number: ";

   cin >> n;

   // sqrt() is a library function to calculate square root

```
    m = sqrt(n);
    cout << "Square root of " << n << " = " << m;
    return 0;
}
```

In another example, we can understand it clearly:

```
#include <iostream>
using namespace std;
// Prototype declaration of a function
int add(int, int);
int main()
{
    int n, m, o;
    cout<<"Enters first number: ";
    cin >> n;
    cout<<"Enters second number: ";
    cin >> m;
    // Function call
    o = add(n, m);
    cout << "Sum of your desired numbers = " << o;
    return 0;
}
// Function definition
int add(int a, int b)
{
    int add;
    add = a + b;
    // Return statement
```

return add;

}

- *Void Functions with no Parameters*

Any function without parameters should be called with empty parentheses. We have to remember that these parentheses are the function call operators, as shown below

Hello ();

In the above mentioned example, the function hello receives nothing and returns nothing as well. It has a side effect, that it displays a message. This function is just called for that side effect. For example:

#include <iostream>

// Function Declaration

Hello (void);

Int main (void)

{

//Statements

……

// Function call

Hello();

return;

}

// Function Definition

void Hello(void)

{

cout<<"Hello to C++"

return;

} // Greeting print

- **_Void Functions with Parameters_**

Now there is another function that can return void type and have parameters. In the example, given below, our function Printints receives two parameters, in integer type. It returns nothing to main, so its type is void. Typically, it is called stand alone postfix as it does not return any value. We have to remember that Printints returns no value, so its side effect allows it to print both integers on screen.

```
#include <iostream>
//Function Declaration
void Printints( int , int)
{
int a = 69;
int b = 96;
```

```
void Printints( int n, int m)

{
cout << x << " " <<y;

// Nothing is returned in the calling
```

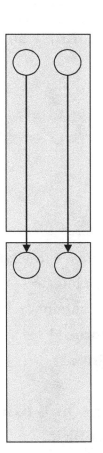

- *Function Example*

Problem:

Write a program which reads an integer from user and prints the least significant (right most) digit.

Solution:

```cpp
#include <iostream>
using namespace std;
 // Prototype Declarations
 int n (int m);
 int main ()
 {
   cout << " Enter an integer: ";
   int m;
   cin >> m;
   int digit = n (m);
   cout << " Least Significant digit is: "<< digit << endl;
    return 0;
  } // main
 /* ============= First Digit ================*/
// This function extracts the least significant
// Digit of an integer
// Pre  "m" contains an integer
// Post Returned least significant digit
    int n (int m)
    {
       return (m % 10);
    } // First Digit
```

3.3 Default Parameter Arguments

C++ provides us with the capability to define default values for the parameters. In C++, default values are used as the initializers. When such a function is called, compiler uses default values to initialize the compilation process. We have to remember that coding of default parameters in the prototype statement of a function provides more efficiency and documentation to the function. For Example:

```
#include <iostream>
using namespace std;
void display(char = '*', int = 1);
int main()
{
   cout << "No Argument passed: ";
   display();
   cout << "First Argument passed: ";
   display('#');
   cout << "Both Arguments passed: ";
   display('$', 5);
   return 0;
}
void display(char c, int n)
{
   for(int i = 1; i <= n; i++)
   {
      cout << c;
   }
   cout << endl;
```

}

3.4 Programming Examples

Problem - 1

Write a C++ program to determine whether the entered number is even or odd.

Solution:

```
#include <iostream>
using namespace std;
int v(int); // function prototype
int main()
{
   int n;
   cout<<"Enter a number: ";
   cin>>n;
   if (v(n)) // function call by value
      cout<<n<<" is even";
   else
      cout<<n<<" is odd";
   return 0;
}
int v(int m) // function definition
{
   int w;
   if (m%2 == 0)
      w=1;
   else
```

```
    w=0;
  return w;
}
```

Output:

When you will compile this code, a console screen will pop up with a text:

Enter a number:

If you enter an even number, let's say 68, screen will show:

68 is even

And, if you put an odd number, let's say 69, your screen will display:

69 is even

Problem - 2

Write a C++ program using functions to swap two values.

Solution:

```
#include <iostream>
#include <conio.h>
using namespace std;
void swap(int &, int &); // function prototype
int main()
{
  int n,m;
  cout<<"Enter your first number: ";
  cin>>n;
  cout<<"Enter your second number: ";
  cin>>m;
  cout<<"Your Numbers, Before swapping: "<<endl;
```

```
cout<<"First Number = "<<n<<endl;
cout<<"Second Number = "<<m<<endl;
swap(n,m); // function call by reference
cout<<"Your Numbers, After swapping"<<endl;
cout<<"First Number = "<<m<<endl;
cout<<"Second Number = "<<n<<endl;
getch();
return 0;
}
void swap(int &v, int &w) // function definition
{
    v=v+w;
    w=v-w;
    v=v-w;
}
```

Output:

When you'll compile this code, a console screen will pop up with a text:

Enter your first number:

After entering your first value, let's say 169, your program will further ask you:

Enter your second number:

After you enter your second number, let's say 29, your program will print:

Your Numbers, Before swapping

First Number = 169

Second Number = 29

Your Numbers, After swapping

First Number = 29

Second Number = 169

3.5 Exercise Sets

- Write a C++ program to print the result in a function. For this, use two sub functions to display results. One sub function would be printing the results, the other one should print the measurements and charges.

To test your program, use the data shown below:

Sr no.	Length	Width	Discount	Price
1	43	33	23	25.60
2	36	9	1	9
3	16	13	12	24.25

- Write a C++ program which reads the lengths of two sides of a right angle triangle and calculates its area and perimeter.

These formulas, may be helpful, writing your code:

$O^2 = N^2 + M^2$

Area = 0.5 *(N * M)

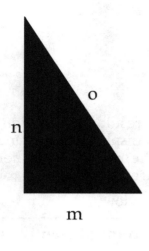

Chapter 4: Selection-Making

In this chapter, we will study about "Selection". Selection is the second fundamental of structured programming. Selection allows a user to select between two or more alternatives in any function. So, we may say that In C++, selection allows us to make decisions.

In our daily life, we face many issues, when we have to make a decision, for example, we have to select between strawberry and chocolate ice cream, or maybe we have to select between black or brown shoes. Imagine our world, without selection, how boring it would be!

So, moving towards the point, in this chapter, we will know about how the selection is made by a computer program. We have to remember that the choices made by a computer are really simple. Computer makes selection in binary form, i.e. 0 and 1. Typically, 0 is used as false or off and 1 is used as true or on.

4.1 Logical Data and Operators

We may call any data logical, if it conveys the idea of true and false. Logical Data is a very important factor in programming as well as in real life.

As far as our lives are concerned, sometimes, we have to make tough choices, based upon logical data, i.e. true or false. For example, let us say, if someone calls you and asks you, "Are you at home?". You would have two choices, "Yes! I am home" or "No! I am not." This would lie under 0 (false) and 1 (true), in programming.

In programming, we may ask, if variable "n" is greater than "m". The answer would be 0 (No) or 1 (yes).

- *Logical Data in C++*

In C++, we may represent logical data in two manners. Firstly, we may use boolean data (bool) with constant identifiers, true and false. On the other hand, we may use other data types, such as integers (int) and characters (char) to represent logical data. If an item is zero among the data, it would be considered as false.

- *Logical Operators*

In C++, usually we have three logical operators. We can use them to combine and create logical values such as not, or and and. These operators are shown in table below:

Operator	Demonstration
!	not
&&	Logical and
||	Logical or

- **Not Operator**

It is a unary operator. Not operator "!" changes a 1 (true) value to 0 (false) or a 0 (false) to 1 (true).

- **And Operator**

It is binary operator. And operator is a binary operator, so that, it has four distinct possible combinations of values. In this operator, the resulting value is true only if both operands are true.

- **Or Operator**

Or Operator "||" is also a binary operator. Like and operator, or operator also has four possibilities. But in this operator's case, the result would be false, only if both operands are false.

To understand these operators use in C++, we may use these tables below

Not operator "!"

Logical

n	!n
false	true
true	false

C++ Language

n	!n
zero	non zero
non zero	zero

And Operator (&&):

Logical

n	m	n && m
true	true	true
true	false	false
false	true	false
false	false	false

C++ Language

n	m	n && m
non zero	non zero	non zero
non zero	zero	zero
zero	non zero	zero
zero	zero	zero

Or Operator (||):
Logical

n	m	n && m
true	true	true
true	false	true
false	true	true
false	false	false

C++ Language

n	m	n && m
non zero	non zero	non zero
non zero	zero	non zero
zero	non zero	non zero

| zero | zero | zero |

- **Evaluating Logical Expressions**

Compiler can evaluate binary relationships, usually with two methods. The only difference in these methods is about, if we need to evaluate the full expression or a part of it.

In the first method, the compiler will evaluate the whole expression, even if there is no need of it. For example, in the case of and operator, the entire statement will be evaluated by the compiler, even if the first operand is false. Similarly, in the case of Or operator, compiler will go for the full relation, if the first operand is true.

In the second method, a programmer can set a code up to print the resulting value as soon as the compiler knows the result. If this method, the compiler does not need to go through full expression. It will print false, as soon as it reads a false statement in the case of and operator. Similarly, it will print true, as soon as it reads a true statement, in case of or operator.

The first method was used by pascal computer language and the second method was introduced by C++ itself. As we can see, the second method seems more efficient but it may have some problems because of the side effects of the second operand. Usually, it causes because of poor programming skills,

So, now, you know! Practice makes a man, Perfect!

For better understanding of the evaluation of logical data, in C++, we can have a look at this code:

#include <iostream>

using namespace std;

main() {

　int n = 5;

```cpp
    int m = 20;
    int o;
    if(n && m)
{
    cout << "For line 1 - Condition is true"<< endl ;
}
    if(n || m)
{
    cout << "For line 2 - Condition is true"<< endl ;
}
    /* Let's change the values of n and m */
    n = 0;
    m = 10;
    if(n && m)
{
    cout << "For line 3 - Condition is true"<< endl ;
}
    else
{
    cout << "For line 4 - Condition is not true"<< endl ;
}
    if(!(n && m))
{
    cout << "For line 5 - Condition is true"<< endl ;
}
    return 0;
```

}
- *Relation Operators*

In C++, we have six relational operators to support logical relationships. All of them are binary operators that can accept two operands and can compare them.

Operator	Meaning
<	Less than
<=	Less than or equal to
>	Greater than
>=	Greater than or equal
==	Equals to
!=	Not Equals

We have to remember that every operator among them is the complement of another, for example if we want to evaluate an expression involving not and less than expression, we may use greater than and equal to operators, instead of that. We can understand this relation using this table.

Original	Simplified
! (n < m)	n >= m
! (n > m)	n <= m
! (n != m)	n == m

! (n <= m)	n > m
! (n >= m)	n < m
! (n == m)	n != m

Now, just look at a simple program to understand it, according to C++

```cpp
#include<iostream>
using namespace std;
int main()
{
  int n=10,m=20,o=10;
  if(n>m)
    cout<<"n is greater"<<endl;
  if(n<m)
    cout<<"n is smaller"<<endl;
  if(n<=o)
    cout<<"n is less than or equal to m"<<endl;
  if(n>=m)
    cout<<"n is less than or equal to m"<<endl;
  return 0;
}
```

4.2 Two Way Selection

Usually, any decision statement in a computer is known as two way selection. Decision is presented to the computer, a conditional statement and computer can answer it as true or false.

In such conditions, if the answer is true, an action or a set of actions is performed. On the other hand, if the answer is false, different action or set of actions is performed.

- *If, Else*

In C++, two way selection is implemented with an if else statement. If else statement is a statement, used to make selection between two alternatives. It is coded as

If (expression)

{

Statements

}

Else

{

Statements

}

Here are some points, we have to keep in mind about if else statements:

- The expression after if statement must be closed in parentheses.
- We don't need semicolon for the statements in if else statements.
- In if else, expressions can have side effects.
- Both if and else statements can be any statement, ornull statement.
- Among if and else only one statement can be true at a time
- ***Rules for If Else statements***

The first rule, as mentioned earlier is that the expression in if else statement should be closed in parentheses. Second rule is so simple but it can cause a lot of problems. To explain that rule, we have to look at the example below.

```
if (n == 69)
N++;
else
n--;
```

In this example, each action that is to be performed is a single statement that simply adds or subtracts 1 from the variable n. The rule is; we have to remember that the semicolons in above mentioned statements belong to arithmetic statements, not to if or else.

Third rule, we are going to discuss, is a bit more complex. In C++, it's a common activity to code expressions having side effects, for example, most of the times data is coded that have side effects to read or print data.

Let's suppose, we have written a line and we want to proceed towards next line after we have written twenty numbers. A simple solution would be to increment line count and tests the limit, in the very same statement. Fo example

```
If (++lineCnt > 10)
{
cout << "\n";
lineCnt = 0
} // End Print New Line
else
{
cout << ".....";
}
```

The fourth and fifth rules for if else statements are closely tied to each other. We know that any statement can be used in if else condition but we have to remember that it is a good practice to use a compound statement for a complex logic.

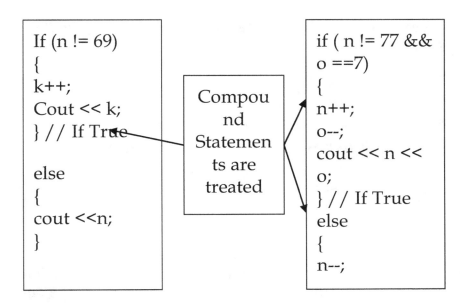

Problem:

To understand if else statement more precisely, we may write a program that reads an integer and prints weather the integer in positive or negative.

Solution:

```
#include <iostream>
using namespace std;
int main()
{
    int n;
    cout << "Enter an integer: ";
    cin >> n;
    // checks if the integer is positive
    if ( n > 0)
    {
```

```
    cout << "You have entered a positive integer: " << n << endl;
  }
  else
  {
  cout << "You have entered a negative integer: ";
  }
  return 0;
}
```

- ***Null Else Statement***

In programming, after taking a decision there are two possible actions. Typically, the action with a false statement is the one that is left out. Letts say you are taking an average of ten numbers, but your requirement states that every number among them should be greater than zero. So, when your program will read the numbers from your keyboard, before compiling a result, it will test your entered numbers. If the test is true or in other words if all the numbers are greater than zero, your program will take their average. If the result is false, your program will terminate and do nothing.

In above mentioned scenario, if condition is not required. So, we can say, if is null in this case. In C++, we call this condition a null else statement. We have to remember that typically, a null statement have only one semicolon, while else statement is simple omitted entirely. For example

```
if (expression)
{
Statements
........
}
```

In C++, false statement can be omitted but a true statement can never be omitted. Most of the times, true statement will always be coded as a null statement. We have to keep in mind that the null else statement is not a branch of if else statement. To further understand the formation of a null else statement, we have to look at the example below

If Else Statement:

if (expression)

;

Else

{

......

......

}

Null Else Statement:

if (!expression)

{

Statements

....

}

else

; // Null Else Statement

Here is a programming example to demonstrate two way selection.

Problem:

We have to write a C++ program that may read three integers from user and print the highest among them.

Solution:

#include<iostream>

```cpp
#include<conio.h>
using namespace std;
int main()
{
    int n, m, o, maximum;
    cout<<"Enter first number: ";
    cin>>n;
    cout<<"Enter second number: ";
    cin>>m;
    cout<<"Enter third number: ";
    cin>>o;
    maximum = n;
    if(m>maximum)
    {
        maximum = m;
    }
    if(o>maximum)
    {
        maximum = o;
    }
    cout<<"\n"<<"The largest of your entered numbers is: "<<maximum;
    getch();
}
```

- *Nested If Statements*

Previously, we have learned that the if else statements may be any statements, it can include other if else statements as well. So, when an "if else statement" includes another if else statement, this is known as a nested if statement. There is no specific limit for how many levels in an "if else" can be nested, but if the nesting level is increased by three, it normally reduces the readability and understandability of the code. To understand nested if statements, we may take a look on this coding example.

if (expression)

{

if (expression)

{

Statements

....

}

else

{

Statements

....

}

else

{

statements

}

}

4.3 Multiway Selection

Many programming languages provides us another selection method, i.e. multi way selection. This allows a program to choose among many alternatives.

In C++, there are two major ways to apply multi way selection. First method is known as switch statement, other is known as else if statement. Switch statement is applicable only when the selection reduces to an integral value or expression. Moving forward, most of the times, selection is based upon the range of values. In this case, the condition is not integral and we use else if in this scenario.

- *The Switch Statement*

Switch statement is composite statement used to make a decision between many statements. In this case, the selection condition must be in integral type. For this statement, any expression can be used but unary expression is the most common.

Switch expression have conditions that we can evaluate for every possible value that can be the result from this condition, separate case constants are defined. With every case, there are one or more associated statements.

To understand switch statement, we may see the following syntax

Switch (expression)

{

case constant - 1 : statement

    ....

    statement

case constant - 2 : statement

    ....

                    statement

case constant - n : statement

                    ....

                    statement

default   : statement

                    ....

                    statement

} // End Switch

- *Else If Statement*

Switch statement works, when and only when the case values are integers. We will need else if statement if we need a multi way selection in a non integer data. C++ has no concepts of "else if statements" in it. It is a programming style, basically.

In "else if statement", we code else if on a single line and align it with a previous if statement. The syntax for this style looks something like

If (n >= 90)

   discount = 'V';

Else if (n >= 80)

   discount = 'K';

We have to remember that else if statement is only used when the same basic expression is being evaluated.

In C++, else if is an artificial construct, that is only used when

- The selection variable is a non integer
- The same variable is being tested in the expression.

- *Example Program*

Problem:

Write a C++ program that reads an integer value from 0 to 99999 and prints the amount of digits, your number have.

Solution:

```cpp
#include <iostream>
using namespace std;
int main(){
  int num;
  cout<<"Enter an integer number between 1 & 99999: ";
  cin>>num;
  if(num <100 && num>=1) {
    cout<<"Its a two digit number";
  }
  else if(num <1000 && num>=100) {
    cout<<"Its a three digit number";
  }
  else if(num <10000 && num>=1000) {
    cout<<"Its a four digit number";
  }
  else if(num <100000 && num>=10000) {
    cout<<"Its a five digit number";
  }
  else {
    cout<<"number is not between 1 & 99999";
  }
  return 0;
}
```

4.4 Menu Program, C++

Problem

Write a C++ program that reads operand and operator from the user and prints the answer.

Solution:

```cpp
#include <iostream>
using namespace std;
int main()
{
    char o;
    float n, m;
    cout << "Enter an operator (+, -, *, /): ";
    cin >> o;
    cout << "Enter first operand: ";
    cin >> n;
    cout << "Enter second operand: ";
    cin >> m;
    switch (o)
    {
        case '+':
            cout << n << " + " << m << " = " << n+m;
            break;
        case '-':
            cout << n << " - " << m << " = " << n-m;
            break;
        case '*':
            cout << n << " * " << m << " = " << n*m;
```

```
      break;
   case '/':
      cout << n << " / " << m << " = " << n/m;
      break;
   default:
      // operator is doesn't match any case constant (+, -, *, /)
      cout << "Error! operator is not correct";
      break;
}
return 0;}
```

Output:

When you will compile this code, a console screen will pop up saying

Enter an operator (+, -, *, /):

After entering operator, let's say /, your program will ask for your operands, one by one, as

Enter first operand:

Enter second operand:

Let's say you have entered both operands, 2. Your program will print output such as

2 / 2 = 1

4.5 Programming Examples

Problem

Write a C++ program for banking management system. Your code should include cases and selection.

Solution:
```cpp
#include<iostream>
#include<iomanip>
#include<fstream>
#include<cctype>
using namespace std;
class acnt
{
        int acno;
        char name[50];
        int deposit;
        char type;
public:
        void create_acnt();
        void show_acnt() const;
        void modify();
        void dep(int);
        void draw(int);
        void report() const;
        int retacno() const;
        int retdeposit() const;
        char rettype() const;
};
void acnt::create_acnt()
{
        cout<<"\nEnter The account No. :";
        cin>>acno;
```

```cpp
        cout<<"\n\nEnter The Name of the account Holder : ";
        cin.ignore();
        cin.getline(name,50);
        cout<<"\nEnter The Type of account (C/S) : ";
        cin>>type;
        type=toupper(type);
        cout<<"\nEnter The Initial amount(>=500 for Saving and >=1000 for current ) : ";
        cin>>deposit;
        cout<<"\n\n\nAccount Successfully Created..";
}
void acnt::show_acnt() const
{
        cout<<"\nAccount Number : "<<acno;
        cout<<"\nAccount Holder : ";
        cout<<name;
        cout<<"\nType of The Account : "<<type;
        cout<<"\nAccount Balance : "<<deposit;
}
void acnt::modify()
{
        cout<<"\nAccount No. : "<<acno;
        cout<<"\nModify Account Holder Name : ";
        cin.ignore();
        cin.getline(name,50);
        cout<<"\nModify Type of Account : ";
        cin>>type;
```

```cpp
        type=toupper(type);
        cout<<"\nModify Balance amount : ";
        cin>>deposit;
}
void acnt::dep(int x)
{
        deposit+=x;
}
void acnt::draw(int x)
{
        deposit-=x;
}
void acnt::report() const
{
        cout<<acno<<setw(10)<<" "<<name<<setw(10)<<" "<<type<<setw(6)<<deposit<<endl;
}
int acnt::retacno() const
{
        return acno;
}
int acnt::retdeposit() const
{
        return deposit;
}
char acnt::rettype() const
{
```

```cpp
        return type;
}
void write_acnt();
void display_sp(int);
void modify_acnt(int);
void delete_acnt(int);
void display_all();
void deposit_withdraw(int, int);
void intro();
//Main Function for our Program
int main()
{
        char ch;
        int num;
        intro();
        do
        {
                system("cls");
                cout<<"\n\n\n\tMAIN MENU";
                cout<<"\n\n\t01. NEW ACCOUNT";
                cout<<"\n\n\t02. DEPOSIT AMOUNT";
                cout<<"\n\n\t03.        WITHDRAW AMOUNT";
                cout<<"\n\n\t04. BALANCE ENQUIRY";
                cout<<"\n\n\t05.    ALL   ACCOUNT HOLDER LIST";
                cout<<"\n\n\t06. CLOSE AN ACCOUNT";
```

```
cout<<"\n\n\to7.        MODIFY        AN ACCOUNT";
cout<<"\n\n\to8. EXIT";
cout<<"\n\n\tSelect Your Option (1-8) ";
cin>>ch;
system("cls");
switch(ch)
{
case '1':
    write_acnt();
    break;
case '2':
    cout<<"\n\n\tEnter The account No. : "; cin>>num;
    deposit_withdraw(num, 1);
    break;
case '3':
    cout<<"\n\n\tEnter The account No. : "; cin>>num;
    deposit_withdraw(num, 2);
    break;
case '4':
    cout<<"\n\n\tEnter The account No. : "; cin>>num;
    display_sp(num);
    break;
case '5':
    display_all();
```

```
                    break;
            case '6':
                    cout<<"\n\n\tEnter The account No. : "; cin>>num;
                    delete_acnt(num);
                    break;
            case '7':
                    cout<<"\n\n\tEnter The account No. : "; cin>>num;
                    modify_acnt(num);
                    break;
            case '8':
                    cout<<"\n\n\tThanks for using bank managemnt system";
                    break;
             default :cout<<"\a";
            }
            cin.ignore();
            cin.get();
      }while(ch!='8');
      return 0;
}
void write_acnt()
{
      acnt ac;
      ofstream outFile;
      outFile.open("account.dat",ios::binary|ios::app);
```

```cpp
        ac.create_acnt();
        outFile.write(reinterpret_cast<char *> (&ac), sizeof(acnt));
        outFile.close();
}
void display_sp(int n)
{
        acnt ac;
        bool flag=false;
        ifstream inFile;
        inFile.open("account.dat",ios::binary);
        if(!inFile)
        {
                cout<<"File could not be open !! Press any Key...";
                return;
        }
        cout<<"\nBALANCE DETAILS\n";
        while(inFile.read(reinterpret_cast<char *> (&ac), sizeof(acnt)))
        {
                if(ac.retacno()==n)
                {
                        ac.show_acnt();
                        flag=true;
                }
        }
        inFile.close();
```

```
        if(flag==false)
             cout<<"\n\nAccount number does not exist";
}
void modify_acnt(int n)
{
        bool found=false;
        acnt ac;
        fstream File;
        File.open("account.dat",ios::binary|ios::in|ios::out);
        if(!File)
        {
             cout<<"File could not be open !! Press any Key...";
             return;
        }
        while(!File.eof() && found==false)
        {
             File.read(reinterpret_cast<char *> (&ac), sizeof(acnt));
             if(ac.retacno()==n)
             {
                  ac.show_acnt();
                  cout<<"\n\nEnter The New Details of account"<<endl;
                  ac.modify();
                  int pos=(-1)*static_cast<int>(sizeof(acnt));
```

```cpp
                File.seekp(pos,ios::cur);
                File.write(reinterpret_cast<char *>(&ac), sizeof(acnt));
                cout<<"\n\n\t Record Updated";
                found=true;
            }
        }
        File.close();
        if(found==false)
            cout<<"\n\n Record Not Found ";
}
void delete_acnt(int n)
{
        acnt ac;
        ifstream inFile;
        ofstream outFile;
        inFile.open("account.dat",ios::binary);
        if(!inFile)
        {
                cout<<"File could not be open !! Press any Key...";
                return;
        }
        outFile.open("Temp.dat",ios::binary);
        inFile.seekg(0,ios::beg);
        while(inFile.read(reinterpret_cast<char *>(&ac), sizeof(acnt)))
        {
```

```cpp
            if(ac.retacno()!=n)
            {
                    outFile.write(reinterpret_cast<char *> (&ac), sizeof(acnt));
            }
        }
        inFile.close();
        outFile.close();
        remove("account.dat");
        rename("Temp.dat","account.dat");
        cout<<"\n\n\tRecord Deleted ..";
}
void display_all()
{
        acnt ac;
        ifstream inFile;
        inFile.open("account.dat",ios::binary);
        if(!inFile)
        {
                cout<<"File could not be open !! Press any Key...";
                return;
        }
        cout<<"\n\n\t\tACCOUNT HOLDER LIST\n\n";
        cout<<"====================================\n";
        cout<<"A/c no.      NAME           Type  Balance\n";
```

```cpp
    cout<<"====================================================\n";
        while(inFile.read(reinterpret_cast<char *> (&ac), sizeof(acnt)))
        {
            ac.report();
        }
        inFile.close();
}
void deposit_withdraw(int n, int option)
{
        int amt;
        bool found=false;
        acnt ac;
        fstream File;
        File.open("account.dat", ios::binary|ios::in|ios::out);
        if(!File)
        {
            cout<<"File could not be open !! Press any Key...";
            return;
        }
        while(!File.eof() && found==false)
        {
            File.read(reinterpret_cast<char *> (&ac), sizeof(acnt));
            if(ac.retacno()==n)
            {
```

```
ac.show_acnt();
if(option==1)
{
    cout<<"\n\n\tTO DEPOSIT AMOUNT ";
    cout<<"\n\nEnter The amount to be deposited";
    cin>>amt;
    ac.dep(amt);
}
if(option==2)
{
    cout<<"\n\n\tTO WITHDRAW AMOUNT ";
    cout<<"\n\nEnter The amount to be withdraw";
    cin>>amt;
    int bal=ac.retdeposit()-amt;
    if((bal<500 && ac.rettype()=='S') || (bal<1000 && ac.rettype()=='C'))
        cout<<"Insufficience balance";
    else
        ac.draw(amt);
}
int pos=(-1)*static_cast<int>(sizeof(ac));
File.seekp(pos,ios::cur);
File.write(reinterpret_cast<char *> (&ac), sizeof(acnt));
```

```
                    cout<<"\n\n\t Record Updated";
                    found=true;
            }
        }
        File.close();
        if(found==false)
                cout<<"\n\n Record Not Found ";
}
void intro()
{
        cout<<"\n\n\n\t BANK";
        cout<<"\n\n\tMANAGEMENT";
        cout<<"\n\n\t SYSTEM";
        cout<<"\n\n\n\nMADE BY : Faheel Nasir";
        cin.get();
}
```

4.6 Exercise Sets

- Write a menu driven C++ program that allows user to enter five random numbers and find their sum, average and smallest number among them. (Use switch statement to determine among the operators)
- Write a C++ program that calculates the change due a customer by denomination; that is how many pennies, dimes etc are needed in change.

Chapter 5: Concept of "Arrays" in C++

We have been using standard data types so far, such as integer, floating point number and character. No one can deny their importance but these data types can not handle large amount of data, they can only handle a limited data. To learn how we can handle large data in our programs, we should study the derived data types. We have to begin with array structures.

With the introduction of arrays we can begin the study of data structures, as well. In this chapter, we will understand some of the basic concepts of data structures. In most cases, a collecting mechanism is required to organize the data. In the programming world, use of arrays is a common organizing technique from which we can process data as an individual element and as a group as well.

Let's say, we have a problem that requires us to read process and then print the data. Consider our data twents integers. We must also keep the integers in memory for the duration of the program. In the beginning we will declare twenty variables, each variable with a different name. We know that having twenty names would create a problem. So, the point is how can we create and store twenty integers from the keyboard. For printing those twenty integers we will need twenty references to store them and twenty more references to print them.

This approach may be acceptable to twenty or twenty five or twenty six integers but this is not acceptable for a larger data, i.e. let's say 200 or 2,000 or 20,000 integers. So, to process large amount of data we need a powerful structure. In this case we commonly use arrays. In C++, array is a fixed size collection of elements of the same data type.

5.1 Using Arrays in C++

In this section, we will learn how to declare and define arrays, in C++, and after that we will look at several typical applications of arrays including reading and writing values in arrays.

- *Declaration and Definition*

In C++ an array must be first declared and then defined before it can be used. Declaration and Definition tell the compiler, the name of the array, types of its elements and the number of elements in the array. We have to remember that the size of the array is a constant and must have a value.

- *Accessing Elements in Arrays*

In C++, we use an index to access individual elements in an array. For that, the index must be an integral value of an expression that evaluates to an integral value. The simplest form of accessing and element is a numeric constant.

n [0]

Usually, the index is a variable. So, process all the elements in "n", a loop similar to the following code will be used

for (i = 0 ; i < 9 ; i++)

n[i]

- *Storing Values in Arrays*

In C++, declaration and definition only reserve space for elements in the array. There will be no value that will be stored. If we want to store any value in the array, we must first initialize the elements, then read value from the keyboard are then assign values to each individual element in the array.

- *Inputting Values*

In C++, another way to fill and use an array is to read the values from the keyboard or a file. This method of inputting values can be done using a loop. When the array is going to be completely filled, the most appropriate loop to use, is for loop. In for loop, the number of elements is fixed and known. A general for loop to fill an array is shown below

for (j = 0 ; j < 9 ; j++)

Cin >> n[j]

- *Assigning Values*

In C++, individual elements can be assigned values using the assignment operators. Any value that can be reduced to the proper data type can be assigned to an individual array element. The simple assignment statement's syntax is shown below

n[4] = 69;

We have to remember that we cannot assign one array to another array, even if they match fully in size or in type. We have to copy an array at the individual level. For example, to copy an array of twenty integers to a second array of twenty integers we could use the following syntax.

for (n = 0 ; n < 20 ; n++)

Second [n] = First [n]

- *Exchanging Values*

In C++, it is a common practice to exchange the contents of two elements we call as sorting an array. Simply, when we exchange the variables, we swap the values of elements without knowing what is in them.

- *Putting Value*

In C++, a very common application of arrays is to print its own contents. This is easily done with the "for loop". For example

for (i = 0 ; i < 9 ; i++)

cout << n [i];

cout << endl;

In the above mentioned example, all the data would be printed in one line after the compiler compiles the code.

For example, if we have to insert and print array element, we'll use the code

int alpha[5] = {19, 10, 8, 17, 9}

// change 4th element to 9

```
alpha[3] = 9;
// take input from the user and insert in third element
cin >> alpha[2];
// take input from the user and insert in (i+1)th element
cin >> alpha[i];
// print first element of the array
cout << alpha[0];
// print ith element of the array
cout >> alpha[i-1];
```

Example Program (To understand arrays)

Problem:

Write a C++ program using arrays, to read five integers from the user and print their sum.

Solution:

```
#include <iostream>
using namespace std;
int main()
{
   int n[5], sum = 0;
   cout << "Enter 5 numbers: ";
   // 5 numbers are entered by user in an array
   // To find the sum of user's entered numbers
   for (int i = 0; i < 5; ++i)
   {
      cin >> n[i];
      sum += n[i];
   }
```

```
        cout << "Sum = " << sum << endl;
        return 0;
}
```

5.2 Arrays and Functions

Processing arrays in a larger program requires you to be able to pass them to functions. We may do it by passing the whole array to a function or by passing an individual element.

- *Passing Individual Element*

In C++, any individual element can be passed to a function like every other ordinary variable. Elements of an array can be passed through a function as long as its parameter type matches the function's parameter type.

Let's say we have a function, named as print_squareroot, which receives an integer and prints its square root on the console screen. Using array, we can loop array's elements to pass through our function, one by one.

- *Passing the Whole Array*

In C++, if we want our desired function to apply on the whole array, we have to pass the whole array through function. It would be less efficient as it would take more time and a lot of memory.

We have to remember that the name of an array is a primary expression, whose value is determined by the first element of our array. We have to remember these two rules, whenever we are passing the whole array to a function.

- We have to call the function just by passing the name of the array.
- In our function's definition, the formal parameter must have the type, array. In this case, we don't need to specify our array's size.

5.3 Array Applications

In general, C++ provides us with two statistical applications of arrays, i.e.

- Frequency Distribution Arrays
- Histograms
- *Frequency Distribution Arrays*

In C++, frequency array shows the number of elements with identical values found in a series or array of numbers. For example, if we have taken a sample data of fifty values between 0 and 17 and we want to figure out how many values are 1, how many are 7 and how many among them are 8.

We have to read these values, using an array called alpha. We then will create an array of fifteen elements, which will show the repetition of each number in the series.

To better understand this application, we have to review the following code.

```cpp
#include<iostream>
using namespace std;
int frequency(int alpha[], int n, int m)
{
   int count = 0;
   for (int i=0; i < n; i++)
      if (alpha[i] == m)
         count++;
   return count;
}
// Driver program
int main() {
```

```
    int alpha[] = {0, 5, 5, 5, 4};
    int m = 5;
    int n = sizeof(alpha)/sizeof(alpha[0]);
    cout << frequency(alpha, n, m);
    return 0;
}
```

- *Histograms*

In C++, histograms are the pictorial definition of frequency arrays. Using histogram, we may print a bar chart instead of printing the values of elements.

We may understand the concepts of histogram, by going through the following program

```
#include<iostream>
#include<conio.h>
#include<iomanip>
using namespace std;
int findmaximum(int alpha[],int n)
{
   int maximum=alpha[0];
   for(int i=0;i<n;i++)
      if(maximum<alpha[i]) maximum=alpha[i];
   return maximum;
}
int main()
{
   int n,fsize;
   cout<<"Enter Total number of data points:";
   cin>>n;
```

```cpp
int alpha[n];
for(int i=0;i<n;i++){
    cout<<"Value"<<i+1<<":";
    cin>>alpha[i]; // Initializing the data
}
int m=findmaximum(alpha,n); // Finding maximum value of the data points
if(m>n) fsize=m+1;
else fsize=n;
int freq[fsize];
/*
-> Declaring frequency array with an appropriate size
-> The size of frequency array can be the size of the alpha array
-> The maximum value of the alpha array items plus 1*/
for(int i=0;i<fsize;i++)  //initializing frequency array
    freq[i]=0;
//computing frequencies
for(int i=0;i<n;i++)
    freq[alpha[i]]++;
//printing histogram
cout<<"\n....Histogram....\n\n";
for(int i=0;i<fsize;i++){
    cout<<left;
    cout<<setw(5)<<i;
    cout<<setw(5)<<freq[i];
    for(int j=1;j<=freq[i];j++) cout<<"*";
```

```
        cout<<"\n";
    }
    system("PAUSE");
    return 0;
}
```

5.4 Sorting

In the world of programming, one of the most common applications is sorting. Sorting is a technique, in which data is arranged according to its values. In C++, usually we use three types of sorting.

- Selection Sort
- Insertion Sort
- Bubble Sort

- *Selection Sort*

Selection sort is a technique for arranging the data, in which data is further divided into sub data, i.e. sorted data and unsorted data. System divides sorted and unsorted data with an imaginary wall. Everytime, when ever system move an element from unsorted data to sorted data, we can say, the system have completed a sort pass. For further understanding of the selection sort, we may review this code, that prints entered numbers in ascending order

```
#include<iostream>
#include<conio.h>
#include<bits/stdc++.h>
using namespace std;
int minimum(int alpha[ ],int n, int m, int beta)
{
    beta=m;
```

```cpp
    int min=alpha[m];
    for(int i=m;i<n;i++)
    {
       if(alpha[i]<min)
       {
          min=alpha[i];
          beta=i;
       }
    }
    return beta;
}
int selection(int alpha[ ],int n)
{
    int beta=-1,m;
    for(m=0;m<n-1;m++)
    {
       int beta1=minimum(alpha,n,m,beta);
       int temp=alpha[m];
       alpha[m]=alpha[beta1];
       alpha[beta1]=temp;
    }
    cout<<"The sorted list is:\n";
    for(m=0;m<n;m++)
    cout<<alpha[m]<<" ";
}
int main()
{
```

```cpp
    int n;
    cout<<"Enter the size of the array: ";
    cin>>n;
    int alpha[n],i;
    cout<<"Enter the array values:\n";
    for(i=0;i<n;i++)
    {
       cin>>alpha[i];
    }
    //calling selection function
    selection(alpha,n);
    return 0;
}
```

- **Insertion Sort**

This sorting technique is usually used by card players to sort cards in their hands, maintaining a particular sequence. In insertion sort, an element is picked py by the compiler from unsorted data, and inserted in it's particular place in sorted data. For further explanation, we may go through this code

```cpp
#include<iostream>
using namespace std;
int main()
{
    int o,m,n,beta,alpha[30]; //, j = m , n = n , a = alpha
    cout<<"Enter the total number of elements:";
    cin>>n;
    cout<<"\nEnter the elements\n";
    for(o=0;o<n;o++)
```

```
    {
        cin>>alpha[o];
    }
    for(o=1;o<=n-1;o++)
    {
        beta=alpha[o];
        m=o-1;
        while((beta<alpha[m])&&(m>=o))
        {
            alpha[m+1]=alpha[m];  //moves element forward
            m=m-1;
        }
        alpha[m+1]=beta;  //insert element in proper place
    }
    cout<<"\nSorted list is as follows\n";
    for(o=0;o<n;o++)
    {
        cout<<alpha[o]<<" ";
    }
    return 0;
}
```

- *Bubble Sort*

In this sorting, we have divided the list into two sublists, i.e. sorted sublist and unsorted sublist. The smallest element of the data is moved to sorted sublist and bubbled from the unsorted sublist. The process continues with the smallest elements in our unsorted sublist. For example

#include<iostream>

```cpp
using namespace std;
int main()
{
    int alpha[50],n,m,o,beta;
    cout<<"Enter the total number of elements: ";
    cin>>n;
    cout<<"Enter the elements: ";
    for(m=0;m<n;m++)
        cin>>alpha[m];
    for(m=1;m<n;m++)
    {
        for(o=0;o<(n-m);o++)
            if(alpha[o]>alpha[o+1])
            {
                beta=alpha[o];
                alpha[o]=alpha[o+1];
                alpha[o+1]=beta;
            }
    }
    cout<<"Array after bubble sort:";
    for(m=0;m<n;m++)
        cout<<" "<<alpha[m];
    return 0;
}
```

5.5 Programming Examples

Problem - 1

Write a C++ program that reads elements of a matrix from the user and print it on output.

Solution:

```cpp
#include <iostream>
#include <conio.h>
using namespace std;
int main()
{
    int alpha[10][10],beta,charlie,n,m;
    cout<<"Enter size of row and column: ";
    cin>>beta>>charlie;
    cout<<"Enter elements of matrices(row wise)"<<endl;
    for(n=0;n<beta;n++)
        for(m=0;m<charlie;m++)
            cin>>alpha[n][m];
    cout<<"Displaying matrix"<<endl;
    for(n=0;n<beta;n++)
    {
        for(m=0;m<charlie;m++)
            cout<<alpha[n][m]<<" ";
        cout<<endl;
    }
    getch();
    return 0;
```

}

Problem - 2

Write a C++ program to add two matrices, using multidimensional arrays.

Solution:

```cpp
#include <iostream>
using namespace std;
int main()
{
    int r, c, alpha[100][100], beta[100][100], sum[100][100], i, j;
    cout << "Enter number of rows (between 1 and 100): ";
    cin >> r;
    cout << "Enter number of columns (between 1 and 100): ";
    cin >> c;
    cout << endl << "Enter elements of 1st matrix: " << endl;
    for(i = 0; i < r; ++i)
      for(j = 0; j < c; ++j)
      {
          cout << "Enter element a" << i + 1 << j + 1 << " : ";
          cin >> alpha[i][j];
      }
    cout << endl << "Enter elements of 2nd matrix: " << endl;
    for(i = 0; i < r; ++i)
```

```
    for(j = 0; j < c; ++j)
    {
        cout << "Enter element b" << i + 1 << j + 1 << " : ";
        cin >> beta[i][j];
    }
  for(i = 0; i < r; ++i)
    for(j = 0; j < c; ++j)
        sum[i][j] = alpha[i][j] + beta[i][j];
  cout << endl << "Sum of two matrix is: " << endl;
  for(i = 0; i < r; ++i)
    for(j = 0; j < c; ++j)
    {
        cout << sum[i][j] << " ";
        if(j == c - 1)
            cout << endl;
    }
  return 0;
}
```

5.6 Exercise Sets

- Write a C++ program that copies a one dimensional array of x elements into a two dimensional array of n rows and m columns. You have to remember that the rows and columns must be valid factors of the number of elements of the one dimensional array, i.e. **x = n * m**.

- Write a C++ program to modify the selection sort to count the number of exchange, needed to sort the unsorted data.

Chapter 6: Concept of "Pointers" in C++

We know that every computer have some addressable memory locations. In the past chapters, we first assigned identifiers to our data and then manipulated data using the same identifiers.

To overcome this, we may use our data to address directly, but that would mean giving up the ease of symbolic names. So, C++ provides you the capability to work with addresses symbolically. We can do it using pointers.

Pointers have many uses in C++, they provides you a very efficient way for accessing data. Furthermore, pointers are helpful in manipulating data in arrays. Pointers are the basis for dynamic allocation of memory so they are used in functions as reference parameters.

6.1 Pointers

In C++, pointer is not a basic data type. We may call that pointer type is a derived data type. We have to keep in mind that a pointer's value can be stored anywhere on available storage on your machine. For understanding and using pointers in C++, we have to understand the basic concepts of pointers.

- *Pointer Constants*

We have read the concept of character constants in chapter one. So, we know that any character can have a value and can be stored in our desired variable. We are familiar with this concept that the character constant doesn't have a name but the variable has to be declared in our code, with a name.

As compared to character constant, value of pointer constant cannot be changed. We have to keep in mind that we can only use pointer constants, as they are drawn from the set of addresses from a machine. Pointer constants exist by themselves.

We know that addresses in a machine or computer cannot be changed, we should remember that the variables would change from one execution of our program to another.

In modern operationg systems, when the program is started, OS puts it in a memory wherever it is allocated. So, next time, when we will start the same program, it will be allocated in a different space.

- **Pointer Values**

Defining a pointer constant as an address, in memory, we can turn our attention to saving the address. If we have a pointer constant, we may be able to save its value, if we can identify it somehow.

The address operator i.e. and operator (&) provides a pointer constant to a specific named location in a memory.

Everytime, we are in need of a pointer value, all we have to do is to use the operator that specifies address. For example

```
#include <iostream>
using namespace std;
int main ()
{
  int n;
  char m[30];
  cout << "Allocated address of variable 'n': ";
  cout << &n << endl;
  cout << "Allocated address of variable 'm': ";
  cout << &m << endl;
  return 0;
}
```

With this code, we may understand how it works. By compiling this code, everytime the allocated memory will be different but as we know that the variables will remain the same.

Moving forward, whenever and operator is used as a prefix of a variable, it defines the address of variable and when it is used as a suffix it means reference parameter. Secondly, it is to be stated that a variable's address is the address of the first byte occupied by the variable.

- *Pointer Variables*

We know that we have pointer values and pointer constants, we should remember that we can have pointer variables as well. Because of this, we can store the address of a specific variable to another variable. This is called pointer variable.

For this, first of all, we should distinguish between a variable and its value. As variable's location and name are constants, the variable's value can change when the program executes. We can even store the address of a variable in two or more than two different pointer variables.

Moving forward, if we consider a pointer value and we do not want it to be a pointer value anymore, what should we do! In C++, a programmer can use a null constant. This constant is represented as NULL and by using this, we can set a pointer to point towards nothing. In other words, we should use this when our pointer doesn't contain an address.

6.2 Accessing Variables through pointers

Consider that we have a variable and we have a pointer as well, pointing to that variable. The question is, how we would use that pointer to relate it to our variable!

In this scenario, C++ has another operator. This is known as indirection operators and represented as "*".

Indirection operator is a unary operator and its operand should be a pointer value. Everytime, its result would be an expression, which we can use to access the pointer value for alteration and inspection.

For example, if we have to add 1 to the variable "n", we will do this with one of these statements, assuming that pointer "m" was correctly initialized, i.e. (m = &n)

- n++;
- n = n + 1;
- *m = *m + 1
- (*m)++;

We have to keep in mind that in the last statement, i.e. (*p)++, parentheses are necessary.

6.3 Pointer Declaration

We know that we use indirection operator to declare and define the pointer variables. Indirection operator is not a primary operator but it's a compiler syntactical notation. To make it easier to remember, we should make it the same token as the operator. For example

#include <iostream>

#include <bits/stdc++.h>

using namespace std;

void n()

{

   int variable = 69;

   // Declaring our pointer variable

   int *pointer;

// The data type of pointer and variable must be the same

   pointer = &variable;

   // Assigning the addresses of a variable to its pointer

   cout << "Value at variable = " << variable << endl;

   cout << "Value at *pointer = " << *pointer << endl;

   cout << "Value at pointer = " << pointer << endl;
}
// Our driver program
int main()
{
   n();
}

6.4 Initialization of a Pointer Variable

In general, C++ does not initialize variables. So, whenever we start our program, all the variables have some random values in them. The very same thing happens in the case of pointers. Whenever a program is started, every pointer have some random memory addresses in them. In other words, we can say that every pointer have some values to allocate itself in memory. We will get a runtime error, if the address is not properly allocated, in many cases, it is because of bad programming skills.

We have to remember that we can initialize the pointers only when the pointers are properly declared and defined. If we do not define them properly, we would not be able to initialize them. For example, if we have a variable "n" and a pointer "m", we will set "m" to point towards "n" at the time of declaration, otherwise, the code would not work. For example

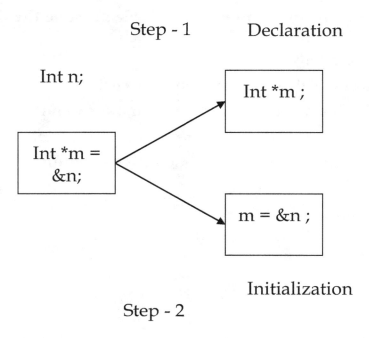

As we can see, initialization have two different steps. Firstly, we can declare a variable. Secondly, we can use an assignment statement to initialize it. We can understand this concept with the following example

Problem-1

Change the value of variables in a C++ code, using pointers.

Solution:

```
#include <iostream>
using namespace std;
int variableN = 4000;
int variableM = 5000;
void reference(int **n, int **m)
{
```

```cpp
    *n = &variableN;
    *m = &variableM;
}
void numberOutput()
{
    cout << "N = " << variableN << endl;
    cout << "M = " << variableM << endl;
}
int main()
{
    int *testN = 0;
    int *testM = 0;
    reference(&testN, &testM);
    *testN = 69;
    *testM = 96;
    numberOutput();
    return 0;
}
```

Problem-2

Write a C++ code using the concept of pointers, to add two integers

Solution:

```cpp
#include <iostream>
using namespace std;
int main()
{
    // Initializing Variables and Pointers
    int *variableN=new int;
    int *variableM=new int;
    int *sum=new int;
    // Reading Numbers from the user
    cout<<"Enter first number: ";
    cin>>(*variableN);
    cout<<"Enter second number: ";
    cin>>(*variableM);
    // Calculating the Sum
    *sum=*variableN+*variableM;
    // Printing the Sum
    cout<<"Addition is: "<<*sum<<endl;
    // Returning Value
    return 0;
}
```

6.5 Pointers and Functions

Most effectively, we can use pointers in a function. We already know that C++ provides two possibilities to pass parameters through a function, i.e.

- Pass by Value
- Pass by Reference

We have now studied the concept of pointers, so, we can use an alternative method to pass by reference. It is simple as we just have to pass a pointer and we may use it to change the value of variable. The only difference among them is that when we do it by passing a pointer, an alias is not created. We should keep in mind that we have to use the difference operator to effect its change.

- *Pointers as Formal Parameters*

```
#include <iostream>
using namespace std;
// Function prototypes
void swap(int&, int&);
int main()
{
    int n = 69, m = 96;
    cout << "Before swapping" << endl;
    cout << "n = " << n << endl;
    cout << "m = " << m << endl;
    swap(n, m);
    cout << "\nAfter swapping" << endl;
    cout << "n = " << n << endl;
    cout << "m = " << m << endl;
```

```
    return 0;
}
void swap(int& a1, int& a2)
{
    int alpha;
    alpha = a1;
    a1 = a2;
    a2 = alpha;
}
```

This code was an example of exchange function. In this example, we call an exchange function, and we pass two variables whose values are to be exchanged.

- *Functions Return Pointers*

In C++, nothing can stop a function from returning a pointer to its own calling function, In fact, it's a common activity for the functions to return pointers.

We can understand this phenomenon by using the following code

```
#include <iostream>
using namespace std;
// Initializing a Function having Pointer as Return type,
int* alphaf(int);
int main()
{
    int n = 236;
    // Displaying the value of variable n
    cout << n << endl;
    // Calling our concerned function
    cout << *alphaf(n) << endl;
```

}

// Defining our function

int* alphaf(int n1)

{

// Taking a Local Variable Inside our Function

int lv = n1 * n1;

// This statement will print a warning as we are returning the address of a local **variable**

return &lv;

}

6.6 Arrays and Pointers

In the concept of pointers, we should know that there is a very close relation between arrays and pointers. We should keep in mind that the name of an array is always a pointer constant, pointing to the first element of that array. Now, because the array's name is the pointer constant, its value can not be changed.

Moving forward, the name of the array and the address of the first element is a pointer constant to the first element, both represent the same location allocated in memory. Because of this, we can use the array's name, wherever, we need to use a pointer. The only restriction is that we can not use it specifically with the indirect operator. The point to remember here is that the name of array is a pointer, only pointing to the first element, not to the whole array. To understand this, we may take a look at this code

{

//Array name is a Pointer Constant

Int n [69] ;

cout << "Allocated Address of n [0] : "<< &n[0] << endl;

```
cout << "Arrays name as a Pointer : "<< n << endl;
}
```

As we can see, to access an entire array, a pointer to its first element may be used instead of using the name of that array. For further understanding, we may read the following code

```
#include <iostream>
using namespace std;
const int ALPHA = 3;
int main () {
  int  array[ALPHA] = {69, 96, 696};
  for (int n = 0; n < ALPHA; n++)
  {
    cout << "Value of array[" << n << "] = ";
    cout << array[n] << endl;
  }
  return 0;
}
```

6.7 Programming Examples

Problem - 1

Write a C++ program to sort an array (selection sort), using the concept of pointers.

Solution:
```
#include <iostream>
using namespace std;
void swap(int *n, int *m)
{
    int alpha;
```

```cpp
    alpha = *n;
    *n = *m;
    *m = alpha;
}
void sort(int *data, int size)
{
    int beta;
    for(beta = 0; beta < size - 1; beta++)
    {
        int charlie;
        for(charlie = beta + 1; charlie < size; charlie++)
            if(data[beta] > data[charlie])
                swap(&data[beta], &data[charlie]);
    }
}
const int max_int = 10;
int main()
{
    int integers[max_int];
    int o;
    cout << "Entaer ten integers you want to sort :" <<endl;
    for(o = 0; o < max_int && cin >> integers[o]; o++);
    int num = 0;
    sort(integers, num);
    cout << "Your Sorted data is" <<endl;
```

```
        cout << "===================" << endl;
        for(int o = 0; o < num; o++)
            cout << integers[o] << endl;
        cout << "===================" << endl;
}
```

Problem - 2

Write a C++ program to sort an array (bubble sort), using the concept of pointers.

Solution:

```
#include <iostream>
using namespace std;
void bubble(int*,int);
int main()
{
    int array[5],size=5,*point;
    for(int num=0; num < size; num++)
    {
    cout << "Enter integer " << num+1 << " : ";
    cin>>array[num];
    }
    point=array;
    bubble(point,size);
}
void bubble(int *point,int size)
{
    int co1,co2,swap;
    for(co1=0;co1<size-1;co1++)
```

```
    {
        for(co2=0;co2<size-co1-1;co2++)
        {
            if(*(point+co2)>*(point+co2+1))
            {
            swap=*(point+co2);
            *(point+co2)=*(point+co2+1);
            *(point+co2+1)=swap;
            }
        }
    }
    for(co1=0;co1<size;co1++)
    {
    cout<<*(point+co1)<<" , ";
    }
};
```

6.8 Exercise Sets

- Write a C++ program to sort an array (insertion sort), using the concept of pointers.

- Write a function's prototype statement, for a function named as "alpha", that should return void type and should have a reference parameter to an integer "n". Furthermore, it should have a pointer parameter to the allocated address of a long double "m".

Chapter 7: Concept of "Classes" in C++

We are using the word "C++" from the beginning of this book. We all know that C++ is a computer programming language. Furthermore, we know that the C in C++ stands for its incestor, programming language C, but what does ++ stands for! This is the question. Answer is, the pluses (++) designate the concept of classes in C++.

Class is a combination of some groups of data and functions which are combined to form a type. However, these classes prove to be more than just types because they provide a programmer with the capability to develop high-quality software.

In this chapter, we will study the basic concepts of classes. Furthermore, after studying the basic principles of classes, we will get to know about defining the class object, constructors and destructors.

7.1 Classes

We have studied the concept of types in chapter one. Type is a set of operations or values that can be applied to another value. In programming, we have declared derived types but we have not been able to define any operations that are unique to the type. Classes allow us to define a type and to define the operations that are necessary to manipulate it as well. Basically, the concept of classes is the one to give C++ its uniqueness and strength.

For example, he should consider a class, named as "Alpha". Within "Fraction", there is some data, especially an integer called "numberN"and an integer called "numberM". We can also add addition, subtraction, multiplication or division in our class as well. We can define these operations using functions, these functions are known as methods when we define them in a class.

When we combine data and operations into an object, we use a very basic principle of data programming, i.e. data hiding. Data hiding is important because whenever we create a data type, we need to make sure that it is protected from any external threat that may destroy the integrity of our data.

- *Access Specifiers*

In C++, we have three types of access specifiers that can be used with class member data or member functions. We will be discussing the first two types of access specifiers, i.e. private access specifiers and public access specifiers.

- **Private Access Specifiers**

Whenever a data is declared private, it can be accessed only by the functions that exist within the class; it can not be accessed by any non class function that exist in the program. We just studied about the concept of data hiding. Data hiding is done by declaring that the data in class is private. We have to remember that the data and functions in a class are private by default. But it is recommended that we should declare it private by using private access specifiers, even in a case where declaration is not necessary. We may also declare a function private. Whenever a function is declared private, it can only be called by its own class object.

- **Public Access Specifier**

When we have to use our data or functions outside of the class, it is declared to be public. We should keep in mind that while public access can technically be declared for both data and functions, the rule of data hiding states that we should use public access specifier only for functions.

In general, data is declared private. Whenever, we may want to access that data, we can do it by using public functions. However, it is possible to make data public. We can do it by using the method of public access specifier and declaring data to be public.

Usually, it's a suggestion to code private members first and public members at last. It has two major reasons, first, grouping all the class members of the same specifier makes the code easier to read and understand, secondly, if the access is specified, all the group members that are following it have the same access until a new access is specified. By declaring the private members first, there would be a very low chance of syntax error or runtime error in your program.

- *Creating a Class*

After reading the basic concepts of a class, we can now write our first class. A class must be declared before it can be used. We have to remember that the declaration describes a type without even having any memory allocation for it. In other words, we can say that the class declaration is just a skeleton of the class, which declares other members of the class.Declaring a class means creating a skeleton to describe and create the class functions and class data. Declaring a class doesn't mean we don't have to write functions anymore, we will be in need of writing the functions. We should keep in mind that the space is automatically allocated whenever the object is created, using the concept of classes.

- *Declaring a Class*

To declare a class, we use the keyword "class" followed by its name. Let's suppose we are declaring a class named as fraction with two integers numerator and denominator in it. So, to create this class, we will use the keyword "class" followed by "fraction".This would be using the same format as we use for every other data type. After that, members of the class are coded in a block. As we studied, we will code the private members first and then we will move towards the public members. In the following code we are including just two methods in the class, the first one is to store the fraction data in the class and the second one is to print the fraction.

class fraction

{

private;

Int numerator;

Int denominator;

public;

Void store (int numer, int denom);

Void print (void);

}; // fraction

In here, the name of the class is fraction. Class name immediately follows the keyword "class" at the beginning of class declaration. The body of the class in enclosed in braces. Firstly, there are private members and then there are public.

In private section, we have declared two integers, i.e. numerator and denominator. These declarations are made as any other integer declaration in any part of the code. It is followed by the identifier and it terminates with a semicolon. As this is a class declaration, it is impossible to assign initial values to the data when the variables are being declared. After the private section, we code the public access methods by coding the prototype statements for their own functions. Moreover, we have to pay close attention to the semicolon at the end of the class declaration, otherwise, we will get a compilation error.

- *Class Definition*

After we make the class declaration, we are ready to write its functions. Before writing functions, we need to know about a new operator, i.e. Scope Resolution Operator ": :". Scope resolution operator is a primary expression. It is evaluated before all other expressions. We can write these expressions as " **class_name : : member_name** ".

Scope resolution operator is used to eliminate every ambiguous reference to the identical identifiers. For example, we need to print a function for our fraction class. At the same time, there may exist another class called print, somewhere else in our program. So, now we have two print functions. We have to identify which print belongs to our fraction class. This is where we use the scope resolution operator.

To better understand the concept of classes and scope resolution variable we may look at the following code

```cpp
#include<iostream>
using namespace std;
class Alpha
{
static int n;
public:
   static int m;
   void func(int N)
   {
      cout << "Value of static N is " << Alpha::n;
      cout << "\nValue of local N is " << n;
   }
};

int Alpha::n = 69;
int Alpha::m = 96;

int main()
{
   Alpha object;
```

```
int n = 3 ;
object.func(n);
cout << "\nAlpha::M = " << Alpha::m;
return 0;
}
```

7.2 Defining a Class Object

In the last point, we declared a class and defined its two member functions. We have not defined any objects of the fraction class, so, at this point it's just an abstraction until we define an object of the class.

As we know, declaration of a class makes a type, we may use class identifiers as every other standard type. To define a variable, we simply state the type and name of the object as

Int quality ;

- *Instantiation*

In c++, defining an object with a class type is known as instantiation. When we defined quality in the above mentioned example, we created instantiation of the class int. Every instance of a class is known as object. As we may have as many integers, in a code, as we need. Similarly, we may have as many class objects, as we need, after once we declare the class and define its functions.

- *Accessing Class Members*

We know that the members within a class can be accessed by statements in the program as long as they are public. A problem arrives, however, when we have multiple instances of the same class as shown below.

Fraction fr ;

Fraction fr2 ;

When we want to print fr1, how do we distinguish it from fr2? We need some way to say "Print fr1". If we were to simply say,

Print ( )

C++ would not know which fraction we were talking about. To solve this problem, C++ uses an operator that is common to many other languages, the member operator, which is simply a period ".". Referring to our two fraction objects, what we need to say is that we want to use the print function that operates on the fr1 object. This is done by coding the object name, the member operator, and the function name

fr1.print ();

Even though the print function has no parameters, we must still use its parentheses. The parentheses are the function's operators. If they are missing, then the value of the expression is the function's address, which is meaningless in this context. This is how we code the statement to print fr2's data

fr2.print ( );

To store the fraction 69/96 in fr1 and the fraction 6/6 in fr2, we must specify first the fraction class and then store function.

fr1.store (69/96);

fr1.store (6/6);

When we define an object, we create only the daa members of the class. The class's member function exist separately from the instantiated objects and are shared by them. Thus, if we define two fractions fr1 and fr2, each fraction object has a separate numerator and denominator, but there is only one store and one print function that can be used by both fraction objects. For example

// First Call

void Fraction : : store (int numer , int denom)

{

numerator = numer;

denominator = denom;

// Second Call

return;

}

- *Using Classes*

Let's write a simple program to demonstrate the use of our fraction class. This program reads the numerator and denominator from the keyboard, stores them in a fraction object, and then prints the fraction.

First, we create a header file for the fraction class. To abide by software engineering principles such as encapsulation and reusability, the class definition and its functions are often put in separate source files.

7.3 Constructors and Destructors

In C++, constructors are special member functions that are called when an instance of a class is created or copied. Destructors are special member functions that are called when an instance of a class is destroyed.

A class object can be created in four ways

- When memory is allocated. Memory is allocated when an object, global or local, is defined.
- When an object is instantiated in dynamic memory with the new operator.
- By explicitly calling the class's constructor.
- When a temporary object is created. We should remember that a temporary object is created implicitly by the compiler when necessary.

- *Constructors*

There are three basic types of constructors

- Default Constructors
- Initialization Constructors
- Copy Constructors

One and only one type of these constructors is called, whenever an object is created. Which one will be called, it depends upon how the class object is created. We have to keep in mind that

- Default constructors are called when an object is created (defined) without initialization.
- Initialization constructors are called when an object is created and the program specifies initializing parameters that are not class type.
- Copy constructors are called when the parameters contain an instance of the class object.

All constructors follow two basic rules

- Name of the function is basically the name of the class, So, the constructor for the function class must be Fraction.
- A function must have no return type. This rule is strictly followed, even void type is not allowed.

To understand the concept of constructors, we may take a look at the following code

```
#include <iostream>
using namespace std;
class construct
{
public:
  int n, m;
  // Basic Constructor
  construct()
  {
    n = 69;
```

```
        m = 96;
   }
};
int main()
{
    // Default constructor is called automatically when the object is created
    construct o;
    cout << "n: " << o.n << endl
        << "m: " << o.m;
    return 1;
}
```

- *Destructors*

Destructors are the opposite of constructors. They are used when an object dies, either because it's no longer in scope or because it has been deleted. In general, we will not need destructors. When an object has pointers to dynamic memory that must also be released, however, destructors are necessary because destroying pointers doesn't release the memory. If enough objects, with dynamic memory are temporarily created, such as when we pass it by value, or when we return it, dynamic memory can instantly become exhausted.

Like constructors, destructors must carry the same identifier as the class. Unlinke constructors, there is only one destructor function because destructors can have no parameters. To separate them from constructors, destructors are prefixed with a tilde sign "~". We may understand the concept of destructors by going through this code.

```cpp
#include<iostream>
#include<conio.h>
using namespace std;
class AlphaClass
{
public:
  AlphaClass()
  {
     cout << "Constructor of the AlphaClass : Object Created"<<endl;
  }
  // Destructor for the AlphaClass
  ~AlphaClass()
  {
     cout << "Destructor of the AlphaClass : Object Destroyed"<<endl;
  }
};
int main ()
{
    AlphaClass des;
    getch();
    return 0;
}
```

7.4 Programming Examples

Problem - 1

Write a program to show the working of classes and objects in C++ programming.

Solution:

```cpp
#include <iostream>
#include<conio.h>
using namespace std;
class boy
{
    public:
    string name;
    int number;
};
int main()
{
    boy obj;
    cout << "Enter the Name : ";
    cin >> obj.name;
    cout << "Enter the Shirt Number : ";
    cin >> obj.number;
    cout << obj.name << " . " << obj.number << endl;
    getch();
    return 0;
}
```

Problem - 2

Write a C++ program to convert time into seconds, using the concept of classes.

Solution:

```cpp
#include <iostream>
#include <iomanip>
using namespace std;
class Time
{
  private:
    int seconds;
    int hour,minute,second;
  public:
    void getTime(void);
    void convertIntoSeconds(void);
    void displayTime(void);
};
void Time::getTime(void)
{
  cout << "Enter Your Desired Time:" << endl;
  cout << "Hours?   ";      cin >> hour;
  cout << "Minutes? ";      cin >> minute;
  cout << "Seconds? ";      cin >> second;
}
void Time::convertIntoSeconds(void)
{
  seconds = hour*3600 + minute*60 + second;
```

```cpp
}
void Time::displayTime(void)
{
    cout << "The time is = " << setw(2) << setfill('0') << hour << ":"
         << setw(2) << setfill('0') << minute << ":"
         << setw(2) << setfill('0') << second << endl;
    cout << "Time in total seconds: " << seconds;
}
int main()
{
    Time T;
    T.getTime();
    T.convertIntoSeconds();
    T.displayTime();
    return 0;
}
```

7.5 Exercise Sets

- Write a C++ program that simplifies a fraction. For example, 3/6 should simplify to 1/2. It should have a void return type.
- Define a class called Time. The class should have four data members
    - Hour
    - Minute
    - Second

- Am/Pm flag

Remember that

- This should have a member function to initialize the data members.
- This should have a member function to increment the seconds.
- This should have a member function to print time.
- This should have a binary friend function to compare two clocks and return a structure showing the difference in hour, minute and second.

Chapter 8: Concept of "Strings" in C++

It is impossible to write a well structures and human engineered program without using strings. Although you weren't aware of this but your first C++ program, that you write in chapter one used string. We have been using strings ever since.

#include <iostream>

using namespace std;

int main()
　　{
　　　cout << "**Hello to the world of C++!**";
　　return 0;
　　}

Some computer programming languages provides an intrinsic string type, we have no string type in C++. So, we can say that the programmer is responsible for the implementation of strings in C++.Because strings are so important, however, functions to manipulate them have been defined in an ad-hoc C++ standard library.

In this chapter, we are going to study about how strings are defined and stored. After that we will explore the standard string functions that are available in C++. Finally, we will get to know about the development of a string class.

8.1 Strings

In general, string is a series of characters treated as one unit. Computer Science has long recognized the importance of string, but it has not adopted a standard for their implementation.

Usually, all string implementations treat a string as a variable-length piece of data. For example, one of the most common of all strings: a name. Names, whether of a person, a book, a car or whatever, their length vary according to their nature.

In a nutshell, we have a data that may vary in size, how we may accommodate that data in our program! For this, we have two options

- To store that data in fixed length object
- To store that data in variable length object

- *Fixed Length String*

Whenever we are implementing a fixed length string format, we must first decide what size is to make the variable. If we make the size too small, we would not be able to store all the data. If we make it too large, we will waste the memory.

Another possible problem associated with storing variable data in a fixed-length data structure is how to differentiate data from non-data. We have to remember that values of non data can not be stored.

- *Variable Length String*

A more preferred solution is to create a structure that can expand and contract to accommodate the data. Thus, to store a person's name that consists of only one letter, the structure would provide enough storage for storing one character. To store a person's name that consists of thirty characters, the structure would expand to provide storage for thirty characters.

In C++, we have two common techniques to use such kind of strings

- **Length-Controlled String**

This kind of strings add a count that specifies the number of characters in a string. Typically, the count is a single byte, which provides for strings of upto 255 characters. This count is further used by the string manipulation functions to determine the actual length of the data.

- **Delimited Strings**

Another method to identify the end of the string is a delimiter. The main disadvantage of the delimiter is that it eliminates one character for being used for the data.

8.2 C++ Strings

In C++, string is a variable-length array of characters that is delimited by the null character. There is nothing in C++, except from the null delimiter, that can prevent an ASCII character to be used in a string.

- *Storing Strings*

A string is stored in an array of characters. It is terminated by the null character. We have to remember the difference between the character stored in memory and a one-character string stored in the memory. The character needs only one memory location. On the other hand, one character string requires two memory locations, i.e. one for the data the other one for delimiter.

- *String Literals*

A string literal or string constant is a sequence of characters enclosed in double quotes. For example

"Hello"

"Hello to the world of C++"

Whenever, we use string constants in a program, C++ automatically creates an array of characters, initializes it to a null delimited string, stores it and remembering its address. We should keep in mind that the string constant is always enclosed in double quotes. Using the double quotes, compiler can identify data as a string value.

8.3 String Input/Output

In C++, we have two basic ways to read or write strings.

- We may read strings with extraction operator ">>" and write them with insertion operator "<<".
- We can use a special string-only function, "getline".
- *String Input ">>"*

In C++, we can easily assign a value to a string. All we have to do is to use an extraction operator ">>". Once it reads a character, it reads until it finds a whitespace, putting each character in the array, in order.

We may understand it better with this code

```
#include <iostream>
using namespace std;
int main()
{
    char string[100];
    cout << "Enter a string: ";
    cin >> string;
    cout << "Your entered string : " << string << endl << endl;
    cout << "Enter another string: ";
    cin >> string;
    cout << "Your entered string : "<< string <<endl;
    return 0;
}
```

For better understanding, this code may be helpful in string input

```
#include <iostream>
#include <string>
using namespace std;
int main()
{
  char yourfirstString[100];
  cout << "Enter a String: ";
  cin>>yourfirstString;
  cout<<"You entered : " << yourfirstString;
}
```

- *String Output "<<"*

String output is usually represented with an insertion sign "<<". There are two options of interest when you write a string

- Justification
- Width

Widht sets the minimum printing area, for the string in an output. We have to remember that within the print width, string maybe justified to the left or to the right. In the following example, the first example writes a left justified string to the standard output unit and the second example uses the same example to show left-justified string to a file.

Example - 1:

fsOut.setf (ios : : left);

fSout "|" << setw (40) << "This is a left-justified (default) string" << "|" << endl;

Output:

| This is a left-justified (default) string|

Example - 2:

fsOut.setf (ios : : right);

fSout "|" << setw (40) << "This is a right-justified string" << "|" << endl;

Output:

|This is a right-justified string |

- **Reading String getline()**

In C++, the getline function extracts text from an input stream and makes a null terminated string out of it.

When the text is read with getline, the text is placed in the receiving string and the terminating character is replaced by the string delimiter character. This statement is always true, regardless of whether the text is being read from the keyboard, through cin, or from a user generated file, i.e. fsIn.

For further understanding of this function, we have to look at this code:

#include <iostream>

#include <string>

using namespace std;

int main()

{

　　string string;

```
    cout << "Kindly enter your name: ";
    getline(cin, string);
    cout << " " << endl << endl << endl << endl;
    cout << "Hello " << string << "!"<< endl;
    cout << "Nice to meet you!" << endl;
    cout << "We welcome you to the world of C++!" << endl;
    return 0;
}
```

Moving forward, there is a lot of difference between reading a string with the extraction operator and reading the same line with getline function. When we read the data using extraction operator, compiler stops reading with the first white space. On the other hand, when we read the data with a getline function, all characters, including whitespaces are rad into the string until the termination character is found or until the maximum number of characters specified by the second parameter have been read.

8.4 Array and Strings

We discussed arrays in previous chapter. We are familiar with the concept of ragged array. Ragged arrays are very common with with strings. It is more efficient and much easier to create a ragged array using an array of string pointers.

To better understand this concept, we may check the following code :

```
#include<iostream>
#include<bits/stdc++.h>
using namespace std;
int main()
{
```

```
    char birds[4][15] = { "Sparrow", "Eagle", "Raven", "Batman" };
    for (int n = 0; n < 4; n++)
        cout << colour[n] << "\n";
    return 0;
}
```

8.5 Compare Packed Strings

While working with strings, we will sometimes find out that two strings are logically the same but different on the machine.

For such statements, we should look at this code

```
#include<iostream>
#include<conio.h>
using namespace std;
void compareOperation(string stringn, string stringm)
{
    // This returns a value that is less than 0 (stringn is smaller then stringm
    if((stringn.compare(stringm)) < 0)
        cout << stringn << " is smaller than " << stringm << endl;
    // This returns 0. Here stringn is being comapared to stringn, itself
    if((stringn.compare(stringn)) == 0)
        cout << stringn << " is equals to " << stringn << endl;
    else
        cout << "Strings didn't match ";
```

}

```
// This would be our driver Code
int main()
{
    string stringn("Alpha");
    string stringm("Beta");
    compareOperation(stringn, stringm);
    return 0;
}
```

8.6 Morse Code Program Design

Morse code is the language that was that was used to send messages through telegraph, in the middle of the nineteenth century. First of all we have to look at the table of Morse code.

Alphabet	Symbol	Alphabet	Symbol	Alphabet	Symbol	Alphabet	Symbol
A	.-	H	....	O	---	V	...-
B	-...	I	..	P	.--.	W	.--
C	-.-.	J	.---	Q	--.-	X	-..-
D	-..	K	-.-	R	.-.	Y	-.--
E	.	L	.-..	S	...	Z	--..
F	..-.	M	--	T	-		

| G | --. | N | -. | U | ..- | | |

Problem:

Write a C++ program, using the concept of strings that reads a text from user and encrypts it to Morse Code.

Solution:

```
#include <iostream>
#include <string>
#include <algorithm>
using namespace std;
int main()
{
const char Alphabet[37] = { ' ', 'a', 'b', 'c', 'd', 'e', 'f', 'g', 'h', 'i', 'j', 'k', 'l', 'm', 'n', 'o', 'p', 'q', 'r', 's', 't', 'u', 'v', 'w', 'x', 'y', 'z', '1', '2', '3', '4', '5', '6', '7', '8', '9', '0' };
const string morseAlphabet[37] = { "    ", ".____", "_...", "_._.", "_..", ".", ".._.", "__.", "....", "..", ".___", "_._", "._..", "__", "_.", "___", ".__.", "__._", "._.", "...", "_", ".._", "..._", ".__", "_.._", "_.__", "__..", ".____", "..___", "...__", "...._", ".....", "_....", "__...", "___..", "____.", "_____" };
  string textToAlter = "";
  string newerText = "";
  cout << "Enter your message to encrypt it to Morse code" << endl;
  getline(cin, textToAlter);
```

```
  transform(textToAlter.begin(),      textToAlter.end(),
textToAlter.begin(), ::tolower);
  for (unsigned int n = 0; n < textToAlter.size(); n++) {
   for (unsigned short m = 0; m < 37; m++) {
    if (textToAlter[n] == Alphabet[m]) {
     newerText += morseAlphabet[m];
     newerText += " ";
     break;
    }
   }
  }
  cout << "Your message in Morse code" << endl << newerText;
  int x;
  cin >> x;
  return 0;
}
```

8.7 The String Class

The data for our string class is quite simple, i.e. One string pointer and one length field. The string pointer is created when a member of the string class is defined. While its contents vary depending on the initializers provided in the application code, the memory for the string itself is always allocated out of dynamic memory. If the size of the string is changed in any way, we delete the current string in memory and allocate a new one.

For further understanding, have a look at the following code

```
#include<iostream>
#include<bits/stdc++.h>
```

```cpp
using namespace std;
int main()
{
    // Here are many constructor of our string class
    // We have to initialize by a raw string
    string stringa("first string, named as A");
    // Then we will initialize another string
    string stringb(stringa);
    // After that we have to initialize by character with the number of occurrences
    string stringc(6, '#');
    // Initialization here, in this step, by part of another string
    string stringd(stringa, 7, 7);
    // Here, we initialize by part of another string
    string stringe(stringb.begin(), stringb.begin() + 6);
    cout << stringa << endl;
    cout << stringb << endl;
    cout << stringc << endl;
    cout << stringd << endl;
    cout << stringe << endl;
    // Here, we use assignment operator
    string stringf = stringd;
    // Here, we deletes all characters from string
    stringd.clear();
    // Here, both length() & size() return the length of the string
```

```cpp
        int len = stringf.length();
        cout << "Length of string is : " << len << endl;
        char ch = stringf.at(2);
        cout << "third character of string is : " << ch << endl;
        char ch_f = stringf.front();
        char ch_b = stringf.back();
        cout << "First char is : " << ch_f << ", Last char is : "
                << ch_b << endl;
        const char* charstr = stringf.c_str();
        printf("%s\n", charstr);
        stringf.append(" extension");
        stringd.append(stringf, 0, 6);
        cout << stringf << endl;
        cout << stringd << endl;
        if (stringf.find(stringd) != string::npos)
                cout << "stringd found in stringf at " << stringf.find(stringd)
                        << " position : " << endl;
        else
                cout << "stringd not found in stringf" << endl;
        cout << stringf.substr(7, 3) << endl;
        cout << stringf.substr(7) << endl;
        stringf.erase(7, 4);
        cout << stringf << endl;
        stringf.erase(stringf.begin() + 5, stringf.end() - 3);
```

```
    cout << stringf << endl;
    stringf = "This is an example";
    stringf.replace(2, 7, "ese are test");
    cout << stringf << endl;
    return 0;
}
```

8.8 Programming Examples

Problem

Write a C++ program, using the concept of strings that reads a Morse Code from user and decrypt it.

Solution:

```
#include <iostream>
#include <string>
#include <cctype>
using namespace std;
string engtomol (string, string[]);
string moltoeng (string, char[]);
int main ()
{
    char alpha[26] = {'A','B','C','D','E','F','G','H','I','J','K','L','M','N','O','P','Q','R','S','T','U','V','W','X','Y','Z'};
    string morse[81] = {".-", "-...", "-.-.", "-..", ".", "..-.", "--.", "....", "..", ".---", "-.-", ".-..", "--", "-.", "---", ".--.", "--.-", ".-.", "...", "-", "..-", "...-", ".--", "-..-", "-.--", "--.."};
    string english, morsecode;
    char choice;
```

```cpp
    char repeat='y';
while (repeat=='y')
{
    cout << "Select 1 to decode English to Morse code.\nSelect 2 to encode Morse code to English " << endl;
    cin >> choice;
    if (choice=='1')
    {
        cout << "NOTE. DO NOT INPUT A NON ENGLISH CHARACTER. THIS TRANSLATOR EXCLUSIVELY TRANSLATES ENGLISH (CAPITALIZED AND NON CAPITALIZED).\n";
        cout << "Enter any word to translate, each word seperated by a space if you want to translate more than one word: ";
        cin.get();
        getline(cin,english);
        cout << "Your Message: " << english << endl;
        cout << "MORSE CODE: " << engtomol(english, morse) << endl;
    }
    else if (choice=='2')
    {
        cout << "Enter a morsecode to translate, each letter code seperated by a space. If you want to translate more than one word, have 3 spaces between each word (for example, ... --- ...   ... --- ...): ";
        cin.get();
        getline(cin,morsecode);
```

```cpp
      cout << "MORSECODE: " << morsecode << endl;
      cout << "Your Message: " << moltoeng (morsecode, alpha) << endl;
   }
   cout << "Would you like to continue? Press y to repeat. Press any other key to exit. ";
   cin >> repeat;
}
return 0;
}
string engtomol (string english, string morse[])
{
   string morsevalue;
   string spacesbtwletters= " ";
   string spacesbtwwords = " ";
for (int k=0; english[k]; k++)
   {
      if (english[k]!= ' ')
      {  english[k]=toupper(english[k]);

morsevalue=spacesbtwletters+=morse[english[k]-'A']+" ";
      }
      if (english[k]==' ')
      {
         spacesbtwletters+=spacesbtwwords;
      }
   }
```

```
   return morsevalue;
}
string moltoeng (string morsecode, char alpha[])
{
   const int count=0;
   string tran;
   string spacesbtwlettercode= " ";
   string spacesbtwwordcode = " ";
for (int k=0; morsecode[k]; k++)
   {
   if (morsecode[k]!=' ')
   {
      tran=spacesbtwlettercode+=alpha[k];
   }
   }
return tran;
}
```

8.9 Exercise Sets

- Write a function that accepts a string and deletes all the trailing spaces. Returns true, if spaces were deleted. False, if there are no spaces to delete.

- Write a function that accepts a string and delete the last character by moving the null character one position left.

- Write a program that accepts a string and deletes the first character.

Conclusion

Congratulations! If you've made it this far. We hope that you have truly begun to understand the basic concepts and complexities of C++. At this point, we suppose, you should be able to read almost any code written in C++ with confidence and understanding.

We have tried to cover a fair number of important C++ language features in this book, including some of the concepts of object-oriented programming, which is also known as "OOP". Furthermore, we have tried to make writing clear and easy to understand, and this book includes many theoretical, practical, and explained examples.

In the world of computer science and computer programming, you may find many academic books. Many of them are designed for students, and there you may find some other books which are purposely destined for the developers who need personal advice for how to resolve syntax problems and runtime problems, in the code, when developing a program. If you learn by coding, indeed, in this book, few pages do not have source code for C++, but every concept is demonstrated by at least one coding sample.

The code samples are very well-formatted, easy to read, and clean so that you may find C++ programming easy.

Moving forward, if you are a beginner in learning C++, just read this book out as this book contains eight chapters so that you may have a better understanding of C++ within a week.

Some people may say that this book is not for beginners! Just look at its size! This book is just too overwhelming for a beginner like you!

Don't listen to them!

You should go for an easier one if you find one. Well, we cannot tell you whether this book is right or wrong. We guess that everyone's understanding is quite different. We can suggest that this book is suitable for a person who is a noob in computer programming, but a business graduate!

References

- Forouzan, B. A., & Gilberg, R. F. (2006). Computer science a structured programming approach using C . Vancouver, B.C.: Langara College.
- Stepanov, A. A., & McJones, P. R. (2010). Elements of programming. Upper Saddle River, NJ: Addison-Wesley.
- Zheng, L., Dong, Y., Yang, F., & Press, T. (2019). C Programming. De Gruyter.
- drsh008@gmail.com, D. R. S.-. (n.d.). Retrieved from http://www.cppforschool.com/project/banking-system-project.htmling
- Stroustrup, B. (2014). The C programming language. Upper Saddle River, NJ: Addison-Wesley..
- KOENIG, A. N. D. R. E. W. M. O. O. B. A. R. B. A. R. A. E. (2019). Accelerated C : practical programming by example. Place of publication not identified: ADDISON-WESLEY.
- Lotysz, S., & Helerea, E. (2014). Programme and abstracts: technology in times of transition: the 41st Icohtec symposium, Brasov, 2014. Brasov (Rumanía): Transilvania University of Brasov.
- Stroustrup, B. (2015). Programming: principles and practice using C . Upper Saddle River (New Jersey): Addison-Wesley.
- Williams, A. (2012). C concurrency in action: practical multithreading. Shelter Island, NY: Manning.

CPSIA information can be obtained
at www.ICGtesting.com
Printed in the USA
LVHW112235080622
720861LV00004B/362

9 798656 983686